"*There's Something About Daniel* is a beacon of light for parents who aspire to bring out the best in their children. It is a compelling and eloquent memoir of an indefatigable spirit who embraces her son's special needs as an opportunity for each to discover their inner strengths. Every step of the way is a walk in the shoes of a truly inspiring woman—as she imparts the lessons that make her son so remarkably resilient, and as she finds her own courage and faith over and over again."

—Ronit Herzfeld, LMSW, couple and family therapist, human rights activist

"There's something about Robyn Stecher's memoir that is immensely captivating. She illuminates the most tender and the most challenging moments of parenthood and life. We are drawn in because she writes as she lives and parents—as an open-hearted warrior. Daniel emerges from these pages not as transcending his difference, but fully at one with himself, and vibrantly so. This is 'Operating Instructions' on the Upper East Side."

—David Roche, inspirational humorist, author of *The Church of 80% Sincerity*

"Robyn Stecher skillfully balances the triumphs and struggles of everyday life, mothering an exceptional child and the success of her business achievements. Few people could have accomplished this with such a 'winning approach.' She exemplifies the invaluable lesson that we are all more than meets the eye."

—Joe Moglia, Chairman , TD Ameritrade, Author of
Coach Yourself to Success: Winning The Investment Game
and *The Perimeter Attack Offense Key to Winning Football*

"Parenting is NOT a charted course, and despite the unexpected turns her life has taken, Robyn Stecher is an inspiration. Her memoir of parenting and living an exceptional life is captivating, and indeed, *There's Something About Daniel...* Her son is miraculous...."

—Regina Skyer, Esq. Attorney, Child Advocate, Author of
What Do You Do After High School? The nationwide
guide to programs and services for the learning disabled

There's Something About Daniel

A journey with my son through complexity, life and love

by ROBYN STECHER

ISBN: 978-0-9825974-0-8

Published and printed in the United States of America by
The Write Place. Cover and interior design by Alexis Thomas,
The Write Place. For more information, please contact:

The Write Place
599 228th Place
Pella, Iowa 50219
www.thewriteplace.biz

Front cover artwork based on a photograph by Gerald Lerner.
Back cover portrait photographs of the author and her son also by Gerald Lerner.
Interior portrait of the author by Kathleena Gorga.

Copies of this book may be ordered from The Write Place online at
www.thewriteplace.biz/bookplace

For Amy,
wherever I go,
there you are.

CONTENTS

ACKNOWLEDGMENTS

There are many people who, over the years, have been integral to our journey. At different times along the way, our family, friends, and the professionals we have met have created the supportive community that enriches and nurtures us.

First and foremost, I would like to thank Dede Proujanksy, executive director of The Lowell School, for her indefatigable spirit, for the support and friendship she gave Daniel and me every step of the past eight years, and for her belief in me. No matter how challenging things got, it was her voice I heard urging me on. I might not have published this book were it not for her. Dede is the shepherd for every life that is changed through Lowell. I am also grateful to Sue Price, Ruth Joseph, Sue Klein, Jeff Smith, Cathy Vicital, Linda (Postiglione) De Lalla, George Girakinis, and the entire Lowell School staff, for all the ways everyone contributed to Daniel's academic and social growth and for the sense of belonging and safety they create every day in the special community that is Lowell.

I owe my gratitude to David Roche, who encouraged and inspired me to tell these stories. He and Marlena are icons of unconditional love. David is the best writing mentor and friend anyone could ask for. Regina Skyer graciously provided me years of legal expertise and she listened and offered her counsel for hours tirelessly, for which I am very grateful. I also appreciate her contributions toward the great summers at Summit Camp in which Daniel had his first experiences away from home—those will stay with him his life long. Regina has always been there for us, and she has been a dear, dear friend to me.

Thank you to the small army of academic professionals who have been so helpful: Sue Weinstein, founder and executive director of the Special Sprouts Pre-school, and her staff from 1993 through 1995, for the opportunity and support they all gave to Daniel in those early years; and Dr. Ellen Morris Teigerman, founder, SLCD, Glen Cove, New York, whose vision for creating a school for speech- and language-impaired children created the bedrock for Daniel's early learning and all the foundational speech therapy that significantly altered his ability to communicate.

I wish to thank and acknowledge Daniel's many doctors for their expertise and for taking such good care of him. I never take for granted how lucky we have been to have access to such excellent medical care.

I wish to thank my family and chosen family: my parents who have always been there urging me on as I stepped to the beat of my own drummer; Ashley Wagner, my beacon of love and light; Joyce Gordon, my constant reminder of where the sun shines on the stormiest days; Kathleena Gorga, for listening and showing me where the beauty manifests, and for all those years she listened to my writing and my stories; Scott Linder, the force, for the ways in which he has loved me and Daniel; and Karen Krugler and Barbara Greenberg, who were there in spirit all along the way.

I also want to acknowledge our friends at The York Grill, who have provided Daniel another supportive "family;" Geneva Simms and Mary Cammarata, my early midwives, who lovingly helped me take care of this baby; Ronit Herzfeld, for her vision and passion and insistence that I could do this; Peter Van Nues, for the years we had and ways in which he loved Daniel; Joe Moglia, the best coach anyone could ever hope to find; and my colleagues and clients at DBA, who supported my creative spirit.

Special thanks to Gerry Lerner for his generosity and great photographic talent. Thank you to Carol Van Klompenburg, Donna Biddle, and Alexis Thomas from The Write Place, for their editorial and artistic contributions and help in bringing this book to print. Thank you to my writing friends, June, Lori, and Joan, for the many nights of good storytelling and friendship. Because of them, I was not alone in the process.

Finally, I am thankful:

To Jim Weiss, the love of my life—thanks for leaving the door open, over and over again. As the song goes, "You're all I need to get by..."

To Alan—For all the good that we shared, especially our son, who is the greatest gift of my life.

To Daniel—You have given my life dimension and meaning. In you I have found unconditional love. I never dreamed you'd be born special. I dreamed you'd become special, and you have. I thank you for giving me faith and reminding me every day, in the ability to believe in that for which there is no evidence.

INTRODUCTION

There's Something About Daniel
A journey with my son through complexity, life and love

D aniel means, "With God as My Judge." I didn't know this on the day my son was born. On the day he was born, I didn't even know his name. Within minutes after his birth, we were told Daniel was different. In the following hours and days, I couldn't have fathomed what that word "different" would mean. Having a child with special needs can mean that your life comes crashing down. It could mean that your hopes and dreams are swept under by tidal waves of liability, loss, struggle, and challenge. On the day he was born, the doctors danced around a vague string of words that would help them describe Daniel. The word "disabled" was later nestled in the unnamed genetic neurological condition. I never use it. I like the word "complex." My son is not disabled; he is complex.

Motherhood is an uncharted course. I didn't know who either of us was becoming. I was guided through Daniel's differences to become someone I might never have been, to find that place where there was a wide open space for the unimaginable to unfold. From the first time I laid eyes on my son, I saw only possibilities. I was willing to discover faith in the unexpected, faith in that for which there was no evidence.

I sometimes look at Daniel's baby pictures. I see a fragile child whose future was so uncertain; I see a young mother, protective and fierce at times, but fragile and scared, too. The prestige and privilege of what my life as an executive has brought me has paled in the memories of the first steps of a child who could hardly sit up, the first sentences of a child who could hardly speak, his first school day after ten schools rejected him. We were told he would never read and Daniel won an award for his interviews. We were told he would never handwrite and Daniel delivered screenplays and game show ideas to Nickelodeon. For years, Daniel couldn't speak an intelligible word, and yet, at thirteen, he led his Bar Mitzvah service and read from the Torah. I have traveled the world and seen places and things many people don't get to see, but the wonder of Daniel's intrepid laughter, curiosity, sense of humor, buoyancy, forgiveness, analysis, and acceptance has lured me into an exceptional life. It is not without its occasional pain or challenges for both of us, but it is a life lived in the unexpected—rich with consciousness, led by faith in the unknown, and filled with love.

There's Something About Daniel

A journey with my son through complexity, life and love

CHAPTER ONE

Cinnamon Snails

Daniel had asked me the night before how to make coffee because he wanted to bring me my coffee in bed for Mother's Day. So I taught him. Or I tried. I went through the steps until the sound of the beans being pulverized made him put his hands over his ears. He was shifting his weight from one side to the other. Following directions is not my forte either, and making coffee is a process I take for granted. I didn't know what it would be like to do this if my hands didn't work as mine do. I can handwrite. I can tie my shoes. I can button buttons and tie knots and open jars and cut my food and get the shampoo out of my hair. Daniel was fourteen, and he struggled with doing these things.

When I finished the coffee dissertation, his face revealed either complete understanding or total boredom.

"Are you done learning how to make coffee?" I asked.

"Yes," he said.

"Shall I just leave it on automatic?"

He didn't answer. He walked into his room and put on the TV. Then he called from his bed, "Mom, do you want ice cream with your coffee in the morning?" I went into his room and hugged him, but he was too interested in whatever was on TV to hug me back.

The next morning he approached my room, walking slowly, carefully holding the cup with two hands so the coffee wouldn't spill. He had waited a couple of hours for me to wake up. I propped myself up and eyes half shut said, "Good morning sweetie. Oh, this is perfect; just the right amount of half-and-half. You figured it out."

"It was on automatic," he said.

I guess he paid attention to the important things.

"I have a card for you." When he ambled back in, he was smiling, his big round glasses already halfway down his small nose, his thick brown hair sticking up in tufts in the back. With his chin up he was only four feet ten inches and as he walked toward me he looked more like ten than fourteen. His pajama bottoms were halfway down his bottom and trailing on the floor. Seeing that always made me afraid he would trip, but I said nothing. He appeared with a heart-shaped card that he had made out of red construction paper and had cut crookedly with pinking shears. Inside the sloping trail of words said:

Dear Mom, Happy Mother's Day.
My greatest memory is the day we made the Cinnamon Snails,
And we said that they may need occupational therapy, too.
When I get married, I will never forget you.
Love, Daniel.

My tears smudged the part where he wrote, "I will never forget you." I reached for him, but he had already slipped away. He had gone to the kitchen. I heard the sound of the freezer door opening and the sound of the ice cream carton hitting the counter with a thud. I said nothing.

"I need some heeeelp," he called.

"No, you don't," I called back, sniffling. "If you want ice cream for breakfast, you'll figure it out."

I wasn't going to run in and help him. Not now. Not fourteen years into this life. He could do it, even if I had to clean up the mess. I used the back of my hand to wipe my face. I didn't dream my son would be born special; I dreamed he would *become* special. I held onto that card like it was a lottery ticket, only better.

Daniel's is the voice of reason when there is no reason and the one that can con the yes out of every no. He is the one who keeps the stars up in the sky and the one who points out the harvest moons. He is the one who reminds me of our family traditions like our bedtime talks and the way I make sure all the worries are gone from his head before he goes to sleep. I am the one who listens to the lullabies he sings to our dog, Gracie. He is the one who once a week reminds me we are allowed to watch TV while we eat. He is the one who will try any flavor of ice cream at least once, while I am the one who plays it safe. He is the one I remind to brush his teeth, wash his face, and brush his hair, even when there was no one to remind me to do the same. He is my baking partner.

On cold winter mornings, Daniel would be up at the crack of dawn. He poured through cookbooks on missions to find outlandish recipes like chocolate-covered, apricot, meringue, mushrooms and orange, pecan, fudge logs with Pernod. When I awakened, he bombarded me with a shopping list of what I needed to buy because he refused to go with me to do the shopping. He would announce, "It's too cold out and the store is too far; you go." I would counter with, "I should be the one to freeze, right?" Then, I usually insisted we make the chocolate chip cookies from the back of the Nestlé bag because I wouldn't have to go out and the cookies would always come out great. One day, just so I could see that freckle-faced, big-cheeked, squinty-eyed smile of his, I agreed to make the Cinnamon Snails.

The snails required that we make dough. From the dough we had to roll out strips. The dough was sticking to the rolling pin. I cursed the rolling pin and the flour all over the floor. The rolling of the dough wasn't easy for him, but I steadied his hands by placing mine over his and together we rolled in a rhythm that would allow for the dough to become flat. Then, the recipe required us to cut strips, massage the strips into coils, and then shape the coils into something resembling snails. As we rolled the snails, some were fat, some were skinny, some were big, some were small, *and* we discovered we had forgotten to give eyes to some. It was quite a motley collection.

"Wow, look at these snails. What do you think?"

He eyed them for a minute. "Well, I guess the ones we didn't give eyes to are not going to be able to see. And, the ones who have no ears are going to need hearing aids like mine." And then he asked, "Will any of them need OT?"

I stopped for a moment and realized what he was asking. Would any of them need occupational therapy? Would they? I didn't know. I asked him what he thought.

"Well, if they have trouble handwriting like me, they will."

"I guess they will then," I said. "And how do you think they will feel about it?"

"It won't matter if they are all different, or not perfect, because they are all going to taste good anyway."

The mid-morning winter sun was beating through the window. We sat at our tile table and I looked at the mess—flour on the floor, sugar all over the counter, cinnamon that never made it onto the snails, chocolate chip eyes that rolled onto a chair—and I realized that none of that mattered because we had each other. Or, maybe that is how I want to remember it. Maybe I didn't realize how content I was right at that moment until six months later when I read his card on that Mother's Day. I didn't know he remembered anything about that day, but I guess he remembered what was important.

CHAPTER TWO

Park Slope

It was January 1991. We had agreed and disagreed so many times, and finally, my husband Alan and I committed to gutting and renovating the big old Victorian house he owned in Brooklyn. Once a hotel, it occupied a corner in Park Slope. I thought of myself as a sort of city defector; I could hardly have been considered a pioneer. Alan was the pioneer, there since the '70s. Long before I had met him, this place answered his need for a studio to accommodate his sculpting and photography equipment. Like others who moved to this historic neighborhood, he didn't foresee the area's potential in a real estate market that would one day boom and make them all wealthy. As for me, I saw the diversity from which this neighborhood was forged and the beauty of the brownstones for which it was known. Prospect Park was only two blocks away with its sweeping willows and lawns where we would picnic, listen to concerts, and ride on our bikes along the drive that swung around its perimeter. When I first started dating Alan, there were a few little cafes dotting Seventh Avenue, which was the main drag, but I had lived in New York City for ten years and Park Slope was no competition for that. Greenwich Village was where my heart was.

Alan's house seemed funky and fun and charming in the beginning. That was when a friend asked what was going on with "this guy from Brooklyn" and I had told her that there was no way I was leaving the city. Even love, I thought, would never ever tear me from my dream of living in The Village. But more and more nights passed when I slept in his bed and more and more weekends we were together, jumping on his motorcycle, darting into the city to galleries, brunching in Soho, making a pit stop in China Town for dumplings or the Lower East Side for knishes. We went scuba diving all over the Caribbean and shared a love of good red wines. So, after too many nights of dragging my clothes back and forth, I moved in with him. The house was a hundred years old and I was thirty-one. Through my association with Alan who had lived there for so long, I got to be an insider, and as I walked that block down Ninth Street from the F train to his home, the neighbors waved and smiled at me, as if to say, "Come on, you can be one of us." I started to feel that this was probably love and that, yes, he did have the capacity to uproot me from my decade-long New York City love affair. I felt like I was cheating on my city by moving in with him. But I did it.

If I were going to *live* with him, I couldn't lie there and stare at a ceiling of cracking and peeling paint. The kitchen and bathroom's old linoleum floors were badly aged and coming up. The floor boards had big gaps in between. The stairs felt treacherous with their uneven rise, and the twist at the top always scared me because there was no railing.

We were married almost a year later. I celebrated the hammock in the living room that defined my bohemian forty-one-year-old husband; yet I wasn't sure he celebrated my thirty-two-year-old "upwardly mobile" identity that surfaced with every complaint and comment and fight over how I longed to make this house of his a home—if only he would allow me. On the day it happened, I wasn't prepared. I wasn't ready for the wall of dust that came at me. I wasn't prepared for the men pushing past me carting plaster shards. I slowly climbed the stairs to the first landing. I heard men speaking in Spanish. I heard banging. I climbed the next set of stairs and as I approached the place where we cooked our meals, where we ate and talked and made love, there was rubble. Wood and old plaster and dust were everywhere. As I stepped in my high heels over the piles, I saw the exposed guts of the far wall. I had never seen what lives behind the plaster walls of an old building. There was wood that looked yellowish and rotted and smelled musty from being sealed back there for so long. I looked at my husband standing with the contractor in the middle of what was once the kitchen. He handed me an old newspaper they had found in the wall, as if to offer something that might take the horrified look from my face, as if to say, "Look, this is cool." I looked at it. It smelled musty. On the top I noticed the date. The paper was from the 1950s. I was born in 1958. I hoped it was a sign. Maybe everything would be okay. I handed it back to him and proceeded to our bedroom, which had not yet been gutted. That would be the next day.

A couple of weeks later, I came home from work, kicked off my shoes, sat on the bed that was now in the middle of the living room, and tried to reconcile how this blown-out hole would be shaped into a home. There is a theory that until something has been completely destroyed it cannot be reborn. We had spent almost a year of mornings and evenings mulling over how we would afford it and how we would execute the design and all the finishing work. Alan sat at his computer every night working and re-working the plans. I sat on the bed, often questioning my sanity. It never occurred to me that part of his sleepless hours he probably spent agonizing over the adjustment he would make. Where would the departure from the worn and seasoned life he had carved out here and this accommodation for his young wife's vision take him? The pain of his letting go didn't occur to me. I could only keep telling myself how I had made this commitment and how great it was going to be. I heard his voice, taking charge, giving orders. I wondered how I would cook and where we would eat and how I would live through the chaos and the men coming and going. I told myself the one thing we had going for us was the recipe—him two parts resourcefulness with his quirky homemade solutions and remedies, and me two parts never-ending strength and optimism. As I sat on that bed and surveyed the mess, what I didn't contemplate was the one thing we had not planned for.

Pregnancy is never a coincidence. In retrospect it seemed miraculous, but I conceived easily on a dust-covered night, behind the plastic of the imaginary wall that separated the living room from where we slept. I have never understood how buildings were built. How three-dimensional structures are born of two-dimensional plans. I didn't like going to planetariums for that same reason. I cannot contemplate the cosmos—it is too vast and too overwhelming. I worked in mid-town Manhattan and watched buildings being taken down and rebuilt and it pained me. I never walked beneath scaffolding, never trusted the process of how a construction site stayed solid. And there I was, contemplating the positive pregnancy test results and the dividing and subdividing of the cells that would one day be our baby. It was hard enough that the home I knew with all its familiar problems was gone. Now, a new body would emerge in order to accommodate a new life. How would my heart and spirit grow strong enough to nurture and carry the two of us through the upcoming months?

I was thirty-three. It was my dream to live and work in New York City, but I somehow knew whatever I had done, wherever I had been, everything was about to be very different. I sat there with my head in my hands and prayed.

It is one thing to give up all that you know of yourself to allow a life to grow within you; it might be certifiable to gut and rebuild a home at the same time. With each tile and fixture Alan and I argued over, I was more and more nauseous and I was more and more bloated. I am not sure I cared all that much what that house would look like anymore; I just wanted to vomit and didn't or couldn't. My already full breasts got much bigger and hurt. I got fatter and crankier, and as I morphed into a chubbier, rounder version of me, our home was slowly becoming upscale.

How many days can you say changed your life? The day you graduated high school, or college? The day you moved from your parent's home, knowing you would never again live there? Was it the day you got your first real job or paycheck? Was it the day you moved in with your boyfriend or girlfriend, or the day you were married? Was it the day the dipstick read blue for pregnant? How many days can you say have changed your life? How many does the average person have?

Just four weeks after discovering I was pregnant, I walked into our bedroom.

"Alan," his name escaped from my mouth.

"Alan," I said again, louder.

"AAAAAAALLLLLAAAAAN," I yelled. He couldn't hear me. He was downstairs in his office. I called him on the intercom.

"Alan, Alan, please come, come right now. Something is wrong."

My breasts suddenly no longer hurt; the nausea was gone. I was having cramps.

As we sped over the Brooklyn Bridge toward the city, I rode in silence. I stared out the window, my hands on my swollen middle. I could feel the slight contractions like I was having a period. I was so sure I knew this six-week-old unborn presence and I wasn't letting go; whomever he or she was had to hang on until I could figure out how to help.

The "high risk" obstetrician said my progesterone levels were so low that I would miscarry by morning. That was the day I started to fight for my baby. That was the day my life changed.

CHAPTER THREE

October 22, 1991

The delivery had been uneventful. *Uneventful.* What a strange word for a birth. It was language I later read in Daniel's hospital record. It was a planned, full-term C-section so I never went into labor. I never had the awe, fear, or surprise of those first pains. Those things came later. If I close my eyes and summon the memory, I see a blurry image of our baby being carried toward us from across the delivery room. He didn't cry. He just squirmed a little and let out a high-pitched squeal. It wasn't a robust declaration that he was here. It was more like an inquiry, as if he were asking permission. Then there was a stream of urine arcing from his tiny naked body that soaked the doctor's pants. Our obstetrician was a very proper man. He didn't wear scrubs; he was wearing dress pants. He held our baby out in front of him, at a distance to avoid any further soaking. Then he carefully handed the baby off to Alan, bent over, rolled up his pants, and continued doing whatever doctors do after they deliver babies. My eyes followed my baby as he was being moved around the delivery room, as his Apgar score was assessed, as he was cleaned, as he was whispered over in the corner, and then as he disappeared behind a huddle of doctors.

So, this, *this* was the baby I had grown to love. I couldn't hold him. I was mired in the trappings of surgical stirrups, tenting, epidural paralysis, tubing, and oxygen mask. But I could see the way Alan's eyes went soft and his hands trembled. I could see he had no idea what he had there in his arms as he held our son for the first time. My husband was forty-three years old. He had traveled the world. He had been to Woodstock. He had been through a few things, but nothing like this. He didn't know the child he held, the baby I had come to love long before this day, the baby who danced and kicked and rolled and twitched and slept inside me. I knew my boy as we had hobbled up and down stairs with swollen ankles and a bladder that couldn't take one more step. As I rubbed my belly and sang to him, he had transformed me from an unknowing thirty-three-year-old woman to the mother I was becoming. Long before he announced himself here with that distinctive little cry, I wondered for months what those technicians saw when they went on with their enthusiastic babble that everything "looked great" as they pointed out our baby's face or his hands or his feet in the cryptic gray blur of their sonograms. I tried to see the glory in those pictures, but for nine months I was content just knowing whoever he was, he was growing and moving around inside me. I looked over at my husband and my son. My son. *My son.* I would later say it in a most defiant and proprietary manner, like I practiced saying "my husband" over and over again when we were first married a year and a half before.

I couldn't move my head fully to my left where they sat.

"Is everything okay?" I mumbled through the mask.

The sound of my hoarse voice surprised me. Alan just sat there and nodded. He didn't speak. I tracked the nurse who came and took my son out of my view to the corner where a huddle of doctors and nurses stood with their backs to us, whispering. Alan was still by my side, and I tried to see what they were doing as I looked over the drape where my paralyzed legs were suspended in stirrups. It was too quiet. Then the doctor told Alan they were cleaning and wrapping the baby. His words were few and carefully chosen. He looked at me and asked if I was okay, and before I could say anything, he said he was going to "finish me up." I was cold. Only half of me could feel the pressure of the pushing, pulling, sewing, putting me back together. I was shaking and wanted him to hurry. I wanted to hold my son. I noticed the only sounds were the beeps of the monitors, the rush of my breath through the oxygen mask, and the accent of the anesthesiologist's voice behind me, asking me again if I was okay. I nodded but tears streamed down my face. I had never given birth before. I didn't know if I was okay. I had never been in a delivery room. I thought there would be more noise.

When they wheeled me into the recovery room, Alan was sitting with our son in his arms. Later, I would call my baby "Pigeon" for he had a frail bird-like look to him. A heavy-set nurse with thick, sweet perfume and dark hair on her lip took the baby from Alan's arms and handed him to me. As I lay there, I thought that of all the experiences I had, there wasn't anything like this. Nothing. My baby was very sleepy, and he rested his head on my chest. He had a full head of dark hair and in his face I saw something that reminded me of my Grandma Bessie. There was peace in those silent moments until that nurse moved in and swooped down like a vulture with no warning, seizing him from me. She said as she lifted him that she was taking him to be warmed because he was too cold. I couldn't protest; it happened so fast. I looked at Alan, as if to say, "Do something." But we both sat in confusion. I didn't remember reading anything about babies being too cold in any of the books I had read. As she lifted him away from me I thought I shouldn't let go. No, I shouldn't have let go. As she disappeared, I looked at Alan, and without words pleaded with him. But he said nothing and we never saw the nurse again.

The pediatrician we had interviewed before the baby was born walked in. Someone must have called her. She explained that although everything seemed okay, there were some things about our baby that were unusual. He had been born with only one umbilical artery, which meant he might have renal or brain damage. His left hip was dislocated; he had some unusual features. She used the word "dysmorphic," which I would later learn would launch the geneticists into their uninvited forensics and blood tests in search of a syndrome or diagnosis. She said that an orthopedist would be in to see him about his hip in the morning. This list of things, these words, meant little to me. They floated away like the leaves that fell outside. I only remember wanting my son back. I asked her when I could see him and she said she would make sure the nurses brought him to me.

Night fell. It was time for Alan to leave. I kept wondering what was taking
the nurses so long. Where was my son? The curtains were drawn between me
and the woman next to me, but I lay there for hours listening to her quietly
talking to her baby. I was fighting the drugs, trying to stay awake in case they
brought my baby to me.

Hours later, a nurse came, handed me my son, and said I needed to
feed him and left him with me. I think it was 2:00 a.m. I was swimming up,
up through the morphine as my uterus contracted with labor-like cramps.
This was another thing I had not read about. I felt like someone was ripping
through me from within. I thought I would pass out from the pain of it, but I
had my son. I just had no idea how to feed him. My hands were bound with
tape, shackled by the IVs. I couldn't sit up because of the pain of the incision
and the contractions. My baby seemed so tired. I carefully pulled my hospital
gown down to expose my breast, but when I offered him my nipple, he turned
away. I closed my eyes. I breathed. I lay there in the dark and held him tightly.
I had never held a newborn baby. I know that smell now like the smell of
baking cookies, hot chocolate, or vanilla. I had him in my arms—a fragile bird,
like the ones I rescued in my backyard when I was a child and nursed back to
life. Whatever the pediatrician was talking about before, we would be fine. It
was all going to be fine now. Nothing was wrong. No one would take him away
now; no, now we would just go to sleep.

The nurse came back. Her voice startled me. I wasn't sure if I was
dreaming. "Did he eat?" she barked. It seemed like all these nurses were large
and big breasted and had the same drill sergeant voice. I moved my head from
side to side. I couldn't speak. She reached over and lifted him off me, shaking
her head pitifully. That was it. I had failed her test. I was being punished for not
knowing how to feed my son. I tried to call after her, but I couldn't make the
words. I wanted to get up, but I was tethered, hooked up to all kinds of equipment and two IVs. The nurse who took him away never turned back. They were
gone in seconds. I tried to fight the drugs and the pain. I tried to reach for the
phone to call Alan, but I couldn't make the stretch, and then resigned myself to
the tidal wave of tears that took over and the sleep that swept me under.

The next morning, I told a nurse I had to go find my baby. She said nothing and walked away. She sent a social worker to speak with me. When the social worker walked in the room, I glared at her. She introduced herself and asked me, in the same way that elementary school teachers speak to their students, if I was okay. I didn't answer.

"I need to find my son," I told her.

"They have him in neonatal care," she said. "Everything is going to be okay. His glucose levels have fallen and they just want to run some tests. Let's talk." She moved closer to me.

"No, no, I don't want to talk." My voice was wavering. "I just want to see my baby."

"They—are—just—running—some—tests," she said slowly and calculatingly as if she were speaking to a feral animal.

"What kind of tests?" I demanded.

"I can try to find out for you," she said.

"No. NO! I am his mother and I will find out." Except, I couldn't move from my bed.

I closed my eyes, and the tears started.

She sat in silence, her hands folded on her lap.

"Can you please, please, get me to my baby?" I whispered.

She asked if I had spoken with our pediatrician. No. I needed to call her. I needed help. I couldn't dial the phone. I couldn't walk. The social worker asked if I had her number.

I whispered her name. "Please, call her. *Please.*"

Later that morning, I wheeled myself toward the double doors marked NICU—otherwise known as the Neonatal Intensive Care Unit. The bright lights, the way it smelled, the energy level, everything about it was intense. I guess that is why it is called intensive care. I surveyed the bays of little plastic houses. I tried not to look too closely at any of them. The babies were too small. Too many tubes and ventilators and IVs coming and going from them, and there was the whooshing and the beeping, all keeping time, pushing back at what seemed like death's waiting door. Then, I saw him. A needle was protruding from his small forehead. He was crying. His little body was jerking and jolting. I didn't know if he felt pain or rage or maybe loneliness. My heart felt like someone had torn through it with a rusty knife. He wore only a disposable diaper. I had so many baby outfits at home. There was no blanket covering him. My first thought was that I needed to get him out of there. He should be asleep in his new crib with the dancing bears overhead. I needed to find out who was in charge. I looked around but everyone was very busy. There was no one to ask. I started to cry. I could only imagine picking him up and carrying him out of there, but I couldn't stand up. I wasn't sure if it was okay, but I reached into the hole where I could touch him.

I spoke to him. "It's okay, baby. It's okay. I'll get you out of there. Don't cry."

I looked down at the IV needle taped to my hand. I didn't even know his name, but he knew me. His tiny finger wrapped itself around mine. I don't know how long I was there. A nurse came over and reached in to check something. She barely looked at me. I started to speak, but I couldn't form the words. I just sat there in the wheelchair in silence for a long time crying and staring at him. Another nurse came over and put her hand on my shoulder.

"It'll be okay," she said.

It was a new definition for "okay."

The rules were set by the presiding neonatologist. Meetings with him were arranged by request in advance, and they were very few and far between. He was busy saving the lives of *his* babies, and this was *his* unit. I learned early on the nurses did what he said; they couldn't and wouldn't answer questions. "I'll ask," was the usual response. He gave the orders. They were dutiful. I didn't understand how housing my son in a little plastic world devoid of his mother's contact could have been helping him.

Whenever I could, I wheeled or walked down the hall dragging my IV pole, as if someone would take pity on me and let me in to see him, to touch him, to hold him. I sometimes stood outside the door for an hour hoping the nurses would let me in early. I wanted to feed him *my* milk. I begged them not to give him formula. But I soon learned breast milk production and stress are not compatible. I battled with the evil pump that pinched and hurt. I would limp down the hall with my meager offerings hoping to impress the nurses, but they were too busy to notice me. They couldn't stop and talk. They pointed to the fridge where I was supposed to deposit the milk, and I would stand there stalling so I could be closer to him. If someone did see me standing there, the usual response was, "Visiting hours are over. You can come back in the morning." I would force a smile and limp back to my room.

In the days that followed, we learned about O2 levels, blue episodes, and bilirubin—terms and labels that I had not read in any of my child-rearing books. I stood by while my son's heels were pricked five times a day, while his monitors were checked. Sometimes they took him for CAT scans and MRIs and I didn't know where he was or who was holding him. I tried not to think about him crying. I thought my heart would stop, but maybe it forgot its pain so that it could just keep beating.

Five days later when I was told I had to leave the hospital, I didn't realize the nurses meant that my son wasn't going home with me. I closed my eyes and prayed for the strength to walk away, but at that moment nothing and no one could have wrenched me from his side. Later, I lay in my bed at home and asked a God I had forgotten if it were possible for this child of mine to know that even though it felt like I was far away, I was right there. I prayed that somehow, somehow, my son would know I didn't really leave him.

Eleven days after he was born, we were told we could take our son home, but we had to name him. And so he became Daniel—the courageous one who walked into the lion's den. A middle name never occurred to us. We dressed him in his blue knit outfit, its little feet still too long and its arms flapping by his sides, and carried him outside to freedom. It must feel exactly that way when a prisoner is released from incarceration. And although we would no longer be at the mercy of the NICU staff, we were stumbling into territory that no book could have prepared us for. Beneath the blue outfit, there was a harness for his dislocated hip that required retraining to move it back into its socket. Taped to his chest was an apnea monitor that would wake us and warn us of his irregular breathing. He still didn't eat all that well, and cried a lot. He was still tiny and yellow from jaundice. As we carried him into the house, I imagined that soon it would be filled with the joyful sounds of our baby. I wasn't prepared for the colicky days and the night terrors, the ear infections and the crying.

I often wonder what compelled me to get up on that first day after giving birth. If the nurses hadn't brought me a wheelchair, I would have crawled down that hallway. What kept me from staying in that bed, asking for more drugs, putting my head down, and refusing to get up? Why do some mothers feel nothing for their young in those first weeks? Why does a penguin risk its life to covet an egg in sub-zero Antarctic conditions? I have no idea. I had no idea what was happening in the world. I had no idea what important events were reported in the papers on the day my son was born. I had no idea what was happening at work, who had called, or who had wanted to visit. I didn't know whether it was night or day, or what day it was. I had no idea of those things. But I knew one thing. There is no evidence that a caterpillar will ever become a butterfly. No, there is no evidence, but after crawling onto a branch and wrapping itself in a magical blanket, when it is ready, the butterfly emerges in flight. That is all I knew.

CHAPTER FOUR

Looking Back

It was February 2007. I arrived at the Bob Hope Airport in Los Angeles in a black town car with dark windows. My driver opened my door. As I stepped out of the car into the heat, he took my hand to steady me. He helped to check my bags and then he said, "Is there anything else m'am?"

"No, thanks. Have a great day," I said.

He is one of many drivers who have come and gone from my life. He left me at the check-in counter. My black sweater, black jeans, and black boots hinted that I am from New York. A man walked by and said softly, "You look beautiful."

The counter clerk helping me said, "You probably hear that all the time."

I said nothing. I smiled and tipped him. I often feel my life is not what it looks like.

I was on my way home to New York. The gate was crowded. On the floor nearby, there were two young children playing a game of baby tag, one crawling as fast he could away from the other who was trying to catch him. Their laughter was the best thing I had heard all day. I sat with my laptop open and cell phone nearby. I typed with one hand while I held a cup of coffee in the other. I joined an audience watching the two toddlers, their parents smiling in delight at the competition. Had I ever had anything in common with these young families?

My cell phone rang.

"Hi, honey."

"Hi, Mom."

"How's it going?"

"Good. When will you be home?"

"Around nine tonight."

"Why so late?"

"Because that's how long it takes to get there. What are you doing?"

"Nothing much. I love you."

"I love you, too, Daniel."

"I have a good idea for my game show."

"Okay, Dan, when I get home you can tell me about it, okay?"

"No, no, I want to just tell you one thing now."

"Dan, honey, we are going to board the plane in a minute and it's hard for me to listen now, can you please tell me when I see you? It will be so much better, okay?"

"Okay, bye."

"Bye, honey. I love you."

Of course I wanted to hear it all. There wasn't one word I didn't want to hear. I couldn't wait to get home.

It had been fifteen years since my son was a baby. At one time, my suits had hung unworn—a testimony to my interrupted career. I spent those days pushing Daniel's stroller in pursuit of what it would seem "typical" people did with their children. When Daniel was four months old, I returned to work because we needed the income. I tried balancing my job and raising this child, but I would leave for work and feel I was betraying my son. I had negotiated a twenty-five-hour work week, but my commute was an hour in each direction and it was exhausting me. I passed on dinners and work-related outings, only to rush home to yet another job, which demanded not only my energy and love, but my ability to research and troubleshoot. At thirty-three, I was being pulled further and further away from the career that once made me proud. I worked for a prestigious talent agency, but my longing to rise to the top of my profession faded as the months passed. Other mothers could revel in their children's growth; I made excuses for my son's slow development. I lay in bed at night, flipping through child development books. My son didn't look like other children, he didn't have a roly-poly face, his head seemed too heavy for his neck. He was plagued by ear infections that would clear and reappear. Instead of creeping, he rolled, and instead of crawling, he dragged himself military-style across the floor. Over and over I told myself, "He'll be fine; he will outgrow all of this." I often questioned if I were home how I would affect a change on his development. I was his mother; I could do what no nanny could do.

Daniel never crawled on the floor at an airport. The parents of those babies playing nearby probably didn't know what it feels like to have a child old enough to walk, who didn't walk. They probably didn't know how it feels to wait and wait long past the "normal developmental age" for those first steps. They might never know what it feels like to have a child whose only spoken words were unintelligible for years.

At six months, a neurologist diagnosed Daniel with "low muscle tone." He said our son wouldn't reach his milestones as other babies would, but to be patient. He said motivation would be a big factor. He encouraged us to help Daniel by expecting him to "work" to get his toys, to reach for something himself rather than hand it to him. It felt cruel at first, but now, I know what good advice that was. Indeed, motivation would be a strong factor in Daniel's later development, and mine too!

I listened politely while well-intentioned people told stories of how their "normal" children never crawled and how they walked late. When people told me he'd be an "early talker," it was their way of apologizing. If Daniel did everything late that was okay. Those milestones would come easily for other children, but for Daniel they would come on his schedule, and after hard work—not when books defined certain behaviors as "normal." The neurologist prescribed physical therapy. It was very hard to watch as the physical therapist worked with our son, especially when he struggled, but I tried to integrate some of what the therapist did with him into his play. The goal was to increase his strength and coordination. I didn't really want to be his therapist. I recognized early on that I wanted to just be his mother. I didn't want to dwell on his accomplishments or getting him to reach his goals; I wanted to relax and love my son, leaving the work to the professionals.

By the time Daniel was a year old, we had assembled a small army of healthcare providers—a pediatrician, neurologist, orthopedist, ophthalmologist, urologist, ENT, gastroenterologist, and physical therapist. We heard so many opinions that Daniel's development would be questionable. The human genome project had not yet been finished. Locked in the mystery of a genetic aberration that no one could find, was the undeniable truth that our son would always be different. With every milestone he missed, with every specialist we sought out, there were no definitive answers, just the weighing and re-weighing of little information. I wondered if somehow I were responsible. I had been so careful. I ate well and I never drank liquor or smoked while I was pregnant. I was scrutinized closely and had numerous tests. Specialists assured me there was no evidence of any specific cause for what was most likely a genetic anomaly. On the day Daniel took his first steps, I had finished tying his shoes, and I backed away from him. He wobbled there for a few seconds before he put one foot in front of the other and tumbled forward and fell into my arms. That qualified. He was twenty months old, and those were his first steps but it would be a long time before he would walk on his own.

By the time Daniel was two, he had expressive language, but he couldn't make sentences. Each labored word of his speech was unrecognizable. A speech therapist explained that the low muscle tone in his face and mouth would make placement and articulation for proper speech very difficult for our son. He constantly drooled. It was getting harder and harder to leave Daniel when I went to work each day. I knew very little about how to improve his development, but I knew I had to spend more time with my son. I was so torn between the needs of my career and Daniel. My husband's business was starting to do well, and while it scared us to rely on one income, I left my longtime employer for the unknown.

When I would take Daniel to the playground, still in his stroller at almost three, I would look for another mother or father with a child who was unsteady, a child who couldn't jump or climb. But the other parents were engrossed, speaking among themselves in little clusters, involved in comparing their children's accomplishments and barely noticing them running, jumping, climbing, or sliding. Daniel could do none of those things. I wondered: Do they triumph over each step, each easy stride, each climb of a stair, or each tumble, knowing their child will get up? In my heart I knew the answer. I kept to myself and pushed my son on the swings. Gone was my community, the place where I was respected. Gone was my freedom and sense of workplace camaraderie. I would have to find other pleasures. I would have to find the joy in my son's smile, in how he sang to himself, in how his idiosyncratic movements, unlike anything in a book, would become his distinct brand of uniqueness. Little did I know how unique I, too, would become.

As I boarded the plane bound for New York, I contemplated the years since Daniel had been a baby. No, there was no label for Daniel, nor did I think there ever would be. Even when medicine could solve its great genetic mysteries, if there were a syndrome or some medical name for this, I would still be content in knowing Daniel is Daniel. That was all I ever needed to know. All those years when he couldn't communicate clearly, I knew his words so well. When someone would look at me as if to say, "I don't understand," I would gently ask Daniel to say it again and I would piece the words together. Perhaps that is where our unspoken bond began—in all that I heard in the words he could barely say. All the answers I would need would come from my son.

I couldn't wait for the big hug he would deliver as I walked through the lobby. The "welcome home" sign he scrawled for the door was better than any deal I could make.

CHAPTER FIVE

A School for Daniel

It has been a long time since I have walked my son down to our lobby to wait for his school bus. At eighteen, he is too old for that. Now, we grope our way through the early fog, each of us challenged by our shared hereditary fate—we are NOT "morning people." Daniel and I grunt and grumble as we trip and stumble over each other, each accusing the other of forgetfulness and being unprepared. I should know where his glasses are, I should remember the money he needed for something or other, I should know what he wants for breakfast without asking, and I should have signed his papers and know where they are. I should cater to his demands and forgive his ornery stubbornness. It is truly miraculous that eighty percent of the time, Daniel is dressed in matching clothes and downstairs before the doorman rings up or the bus driver calls from her cell phone. There is something comforting about the predictable, something to be said for the same fights we have every morning about whether his teeth are brushed and why I care because they are his teeth not mine, whether his glasses are clean and why I should bother because they are not mine either, and whether his belt is on, since if his pants fall down, after all, it is his behind that the world will see, not mine—same for his face being washed or shaven because, after all, it is not my face. And, as surely as I know my name, within minutes of being gone, he will call from his cell phone and say, "I love you."

Watching my son leave for school has always been a bittersweet departure. When Daniel was very young, I watched as his little yellow bus pulled up for him. The matron came off the bus and as he walked away with her, I wondered if other parents thought about whether their son or daughter would be capable of keeping up or whether they would be terrified by a bully? Their children probably didn't have issues with communicating so they could be understood. Their children probably weren't concerned with too much noise, too much sun, winds that were too strong, or by going up and down steps and hauling a book bag they could barely manage. Most of them would never wonder whether their child might be tormented by other kids because he or she wore glasses and hearing aids and walked with an uneven gait, or because their child was simply different in some way—but then, those were not the only things I saw when Daniel left for school. When I looked at my son, I saw what I see today: a young boy becoming a young man I'd be proud of, a young man who overcame and defeated whatever obstacles were in his way. That was how I got him going, or I would have never let him leave the house.

Educating a child with special needs is a delicate balance between finding the right academic setting and finding the best social fit. There are many arguments for and against "mainstreaming"—especially if the child has academic promise but is in need of rigorous social, educational, and therapeutic support. We began the special education journey when Daniel was two. He had been enrolled in a well-known local preschool in our neighborhood in Park Slope, Brooklyn, but after a week, the director called to say that he just wasn't "fitting in." We still had no "official" diagnosis, just the three words we kept hearing, "Global Developmental Delay," which would later become the standard catch-all for his constellation of issues—hypotonia (low muscle tone), speech, and emerging fine motor issues.

It was heartbreaking to learn that because he didn't look or act like a "typical" two-year-old, Daniel couldn't go to the school of our choice. I was informed by the director of the preschool he had attended briefly that we could have Daniel evaluated, at no cost to us, by the Committee on Preschool Education (CPSE), which was a division of our Board of Education. If he were found to be "A Preschooler With a Disability," he would be entitled to attend a therapeutic preschool or receive a variety of at-home services. If my husband and I chose a state-approved, private special-education preschool, then the tuition would come from state and federal sources. If we chose a "non-approved," private special-education preschool, the tuition would be ours to pay, plus therapeutic services.

At first, I was in denial. How could a bunch of strangers tell me what my son needed? I was his mother. I knew him. They didn't. I was sure he would catch up. I was sure his physical challenges were getting in the way of the world seeing him for who he was. I knew him, but no one else did. I kept reading books, trying to educate myself, but it wasn't easy; there was no Internet then and there was very little literature on children with special needs. I believed he wasn't on the spectrum of autism. He wasn't emotionally challenged; he was just finding his way through a maze of neurological challenges. I knew he would come out the other side, but I had no idea then, how much therapy it would take, or how that would happen.

I took the advice of the nursery school director, and called our local school district. The social worker I spoke with recommended that Daniel be tested at one of their approved testing sites, a local private special-education preschool. It was possible that school could accept Daniel if we had him tested there. We were impressed by the school. There were ten children in a class and three teachers. It was bright and cheery and looked like any other small private preschool.

On the day of Daniel's evaluations, the testing was minimal because of his severe speech disorder, and the evaluators were not able to establish rapport with him. Daniel was distracted and they had little patience. I intervened a bit, but they were not interested in my assessment of my son. The experience was gut-wrenching for me. After reviewing the results of their report, the director of that school informed us that her school wouldn't be able to accommodate Daniel; his needs exceeded what the school could provide. Up until that moment, I hadn't realized that even a special-education school could reject Daniel if it were determined that it couldn't service his needs. Daniel was awkward and small and his speech was barely intelligible. His need for physical therapy was a further complication—many schools staffed occupational and speech therapists, but not physical therapists. Any program could exclude him even though they didn't know his wonderful qualities and the potential I saw. I urged the directors of this school to reconsider, but they were unwilling. There wasn't a thing I could do.

I called our local school district again. The social worker was exasperated this time. She had 350 other cases to process. "What do you want from me?" she asked. "I can't tell them what to do!" It was clearly my job to find my son a school that could service his needs. Visits to six more local nursery schools proved fruitless. The one school that accepted Daniel did not seem to have the right population. We sought out a private neurological work-up and some testing. Daniel's high expressive verbal IQ but significant speech and motor impairment were an odd combination. The challenge would be in finding what is called an "appropriate peer group." Daniel's testing profile was complicated; there was simply no "box" for him. The one school in our neighborhood that I felt would be best, rejected him. One day, I saw the director of that same school getting out of her parked car. I walked over to her, quietly introduced myself, and explained to her that I wasn't crazy, but that my son had been rejected by her school along with seven other programs.

"Please," I urged her. "Just meet him yourself. He is so sweet and bright, you'll see."

With trepidation, she conceded. I knew my son would surprise everyone if given the chance. He had so much more to offer than his testing or a brief meeting could ever reveal. On the day we received our acceptance letter, I cried and prayed he would do well there.

Because the preschool was on the approved list of state-funded schools, to officially enroll him, we had to go back to our local school district. At that meeting, the district administrator was focused on a pile of folders in front of her. There was no eye contact. She had her job to do; I had mine. She sighed a few times and asked if we were "happy" with our acceptance. That was hardly what I was feeling. We were at the mercy of a system that felt impersonal and uncaring. It had been three months since I had contacted her and she had done little to help us. I hoped we were doing the right thing. I couldn't find any other school for my son.

In addition to requiring a special school, testing revealed Daniel would need speech therapy, occupational therapy, and physical therapy. This was a very hard thing for me to accept, but as I read and read Daniel's reports, I knew that if I did not follow through with the recommended therapy, I might be jeopardizing Daniel's progress. The preschool that had accepted him was only willing to provide half the hours of services the specialists recommended. I wanted to say something, but I was afraid that if we asked for too much, the school would renege on its offer to accept Daniel. I decided we would privately supply whatever additional therapies were needed.

On that September day in 1994, as I watched Daniel walk into his classroom, I realized that six months earlier I had left my career to be home with my son. I didn't know at the time that advocating for my son to enter *preschool* would become my full-time job! Daniel didn't fit in easily with typically developing children. But, at this school he would have a peer group. Within a few months, with all of his therapies and his nurturing teachers, his progress was encouraging. We became part of a special community. As the year progressed, Daniel's teachers and therapists were able to help him past his garbled speech, awkward gait, and inability to hold a crayon. They all agreed Daniel's unique qualities and motivation to learn would help him to achieve his potential. They encouraged me by reinforcing how much Daniel loved school and how hard he worked in therapy. They urged us to have him remain at school through the summer and the following year. His first full sentence came at the age of three. He said, "Mama, I want juice." It did not sound like that, but it gave me hope. Perhaps with the help, he could catch up.

The following September, we learned we would be facing more battles. In New York City, a child can no longer be funded for a special-education preschool if he or she turns five by December of the school year. Since Daniel was born in 1991, this meant that in September of 1995, he would still have to go onto kindergarten even though he would be only four and despite the fact that he was significantly developmentally delayed. We were told it would be an arduous legal battle to try to keep him in preschool for that extra year.

By then I had come to terms that my son was unable to attend a general education class and we began to explore the special-education options for our son's first year of elementary school. We learned that there were three choices: the neighborhood public schools that have inclusion classes as well as self-contained special education classes; state-approved private schools funded by the city or state for children where public school would be inappropriate; and independent private schools that are not on the state-approved list. Parents will choose to place their child in non-approved schools for a variety of reasons, but most often because there is no space at the few approved schools. If a child goes to an independent, private special-education school, the parents have to sue the school district annually for tuition reimbursement.

The laws and regulations governing special education are founded on the federal statute known as the Individual with Disabilities Education Act ("IDEA"). This law requires that children with educational handicaps receive a free and *appropriate* public education in the least restrictive environment. Although the law requires only an "appropriate" education, we were determined to have the best possible education for Daniel. We would have him appropriately educated by *our* standards. That was always a priority.

I knew Daniel's would be a difficult case and I called our local school district in January, anticipating that it would take district officials some time to prepare for our review before the Committee on Special Education. I mentioned that they wouldn't have to evaluate Daniel because I had his evaluations done privately— this should have saved the district some expense—and the woman I spoke with agreed this was a good idea. By this time, a social worker from our local school district had visited his preschool. She seemed nice enough as she asked me to describe Daniel and to give her an idea of what type of school we were looking for. Our son was mastering age-appropriate concepts, but his speech, motor issues, and lagging social skills would still require a lot of facilitation and one-on-one attention. In a hushed voice, this woman encouraged me to become familiar with both public and non-public schools because when the Committee on Special Education (CSE) made its recommendation, I needed to be familiar with the options.

She told me, "Your son is in a tiny community now and he probably doesn't belong in a huge public school. Those neighborhood schools are so overcrowded and over-utilized. And, the class-size numbers have just been upped so that there are twenty-four to thirty in a regular class and maybe eighteen to twenty in an inclusion class. I think he belongs in private school. What about the private schools?"

I was afraid to answer her. I had heard stories about parents seeking private school special education for their children and the opposition they had faced from the New York City Board of Education. I asked if she could help me gain access to the public schools in our neighborhood, but she couldn't. I gave her copies of Daniel's most current testing. Once all the evaluations were in, we would attend a CSE review. Daniel would no longer be generally classified as a "Preschooler with a Disability." Instead, he would be classified according to his predominant handicapping condition, and at that time, the Committee on Special Education would make a recommendation to us for an appropriate elementary school or program.

I called a private special-education school nearby, and the director educated me by telling me that securing the education I sought for my son would require an advocate. She suggested I meet with Regina Skyer, a New York City attorney and social worker whose primary practice is advocacy and education law. Regina's intelligence, warmth, and willingness to share her knowledge made me realize that I had a lot to learn. She cautioned me to put on my seat belt because getting my son enrolled in a good school with the right services meant I was going for "the ride of my life."

I was a newcomer to this way of life. Why would we need a lawyer or an advocate in a system that was supposed to help us? I didn't know it then, but Regina would become our ally and an integral player over many years of securing the education we sought for our son.

As instructed, over the next few weeks, I placed numerous phone calls to our local school district. All went unanswered. Our local school district is one of many districts in New York City. I was quickly learning that I would have to become familiar both with our local school district, and with the Board of Education in New York City (now called the Department of Education), which was the overseeing body of all the local districts.

Regina explained that the Board of Education was anticipating that we were going to push for private school funding. In Daniel's case, that education could be worth upwards of $50,000 a year including his therapies and his busing. In an effort to discredit our testing, a representative from our district had been to the preschool to evaluate Daniel, which they could do without my consent. Despite the testing I had done, they could have been re-testing Daniel to gather information in an attempt to prove him as "low-functioning" as possible. This would substantially alter the kind of services and class the CSE would place him in. I was furious.

Meanwhile, it was late spring and we were doing what we could to explore the possibilities. September was right around the corner. By then, three of the private schools at which we interviewed, had already rejected our son. It wasn't easy to take. Although we had no official reason, I believed a more typical-looking child might have stood a better chance at the few openings these non-public schools had to offer. Each day I tried to investigate other schools to see, other places to go. It was hard enough to endure the realities of the life we were living, along with distrusting our school district. It was equally distressing for me to feel our son was being discriminated against, in my opinion, because of his appearance.

About the same time and without our district's knowledge, I was finally able to do the impossible—I had negotiated a meeting with the special education teacher at a public school. I felt like I was entering Fort Knox, and to this day I don't know why it was so difficult at the time for taxpaying parents in New York City to view those classes. I observed a self-contained class of special needs children ranging from almost five to almost eight years old, children who were classified with "readiness" issues. After I described Daniel, the teacher said, "As you have perhaps ascertained, finding the right situation for children like your son is very hard in the public school system." I suspected that Daniel's intellectual functioning was higher than those children I had seen.

By early March, we had endured seven months of anxiety as to where Daniel would attend school, and still nothing looked promising. I would have home-schooled him if I could have figured out how to provide him a social life.

When the director from the fifth school we visited called to say they would give Daniel a try and the only financial commitment required was a small deposit, we decided to take the gamble in case no other school accepted our son. It was a private school and we would be responsible for the full tuition, which at that time seemed an impossible expense. However, if we could prove that the Board of Education had not found our son an appropriate placement by its deadline in June of that year, we had the option of bringing our case for tuition reimbursement against the school district at an impartial hearing at the Board of Education. At least we had one school willing to enroll our son. That was a huge relief.

I had to start compiling all the past months' interactions and testing. I requested copies of my son's records from our local school district, but I was told that someone in the office was just about to copy the reports for me when someone from the district's assistant chairman's office took the file away. It seemed like a deliberate move to keep me from getting the information. That same day I also called the preschool administrator at the district to tell her of our troubles. She acted like this kind of treatment was standard operating procedure. I wanted to visit another neighborhood public school, just in case we were not able to get tuition reimbursement and I had hoped she could set it up, but she never called me back.

While this was going on, I kept getting notices from the Board of Education that it wanted Daniel to be further tested. This was so unfair. I requested an impartial hearing at the Board of Education to challenge this unnecessary and cruel treatment of such a young child. The stark office known as "Room 116," at 110 Livingston Street in Brooklyn, was the place for parents venting their grievances against the Board of Education to be heard. Hearing officers who are usually attorneys or judges preside in an environment very much like court. We would be represented by Regina, our attorney, and the Board of Education would have its own attorney.

Neatly dressed and a little nervous, I felt safe next to Regina. My professional life as an agent had often required me to engage in heated negotiations, but as I listened to the rambling testimony from the district's head psychologist who had never met Daniel, implying that our son needed to undergo psychiatric testing, I realized how vulnerable I was. How vulnerable Daniel was. Regina had warned me early on, "No matter who you are, no matter how strong, no matter how tough, this is your baby you will be fighting for, and no stakes are going to feel higher than that." I knew then just how much I needed her. Daniel had been through fifteen hours of rigorous neuropsychological tests and had never exhibited psychiatric issues. No one at his preschool had ever raised concerns over his emotional well-being. He was a well-adjusted, happy child. My battle to protect my son from people driven by bureaucracy was justifiable; they wanted to pull Daniel apart limb by limb, dissect him, and I wasn't going to sit there passively while they did this. As far as I was concerned, not one of them had laid eyes on my son and nothing gave them this right. The assistant chair-person of our school district openly admitted at the hearing that our district's egregious position stemmed from its suspicion that we were seeking a "free" private-school education for our son. I tried to guess how much this hearing would cost. If we won, the legal fees would total thousands of dollars and would be paid by the Board of Education. It seemed an unconscionable waste of time and energy. But what choice did we have? After three hours of testimony, our case was continued—more waiting, more energy, more money to be spent.

Throughout our hearing, while the Board of Education maintained that we were seeking this unnecessary "free" education for our son, not one of their psychologists or educational specialists had bothered to ask about our efforts to see public school programs. This would certainly have proven to the Board of Education that we weren't exclusively seeking a private school for our son. We wanted Daniel educated where he would receive the best services from the best professionals; we didn't care it if was public or private. One of our biggest hopes was that the school would be nearby our home. Daniel was five and the school that had accepted him would have been an hour bus ride in each direction. That scared me.

When our hearing was completed, it was finally concluded that Daniel wouldn't be subjected to further testing. The district had wasted months of time and thousands of dollars to try to discredit our testing by the best professionals in New York City.

By late May, we finally received notice that a team comprised of a teacher, a psychologist, and two administrators from the Board of Education would recommend a special education program, and specific goals would be written for Daniel. This would be his Individualized Education Plan (IEP). Nine months after we began, Regina and I were composed as the Board of Education's psychologist and the committee announced their decision. They unanimously agreed that Daniel should be enrolled in a non-public school. However, when we saw Daniel's Individualized Education Plan that the Committee on Special Education had written for him, we noticed that his preschool goals, which had been written and met the previous year, were left intact. Only the dates had been changed. Clearly, not one of the six team members sitting in that room cared. Not one showed any interest in whether the IEP was appropriate. And still, the Board of Education had not come up with a placement. All we had was the board's agreement that Daniel would have to go to a non-public school and now the board would have to find him one. We had not disclosed that we had a letter of acceptance, as the burden was on them to find an "accepted state-funded" school. Besides, the school we had found wasn't on the approved list.

Time was running out. Daniel had already been rejected by four of the accepted state-funded schools we had pursued. Because we didn't trust that the Board of Education would come through with an accepted school by September, we decided to enroll Daniel in the only school that had accepted him. Because it was a private school, we would be required to pay the full tuition out-of-pocket and we would have to go back to another impartial hearing for funding. This was terrifying, but Regina was confident we would win.

Weeks before school was to start, I had started calling the district to arrange for a bus—because even though this was a private school of my choice, the Board of Education was obligated to supply busing. The thought of my son traveling an hour to and from school each day was very stressful, but I had learned that there were a few other young Brooklyn children going to the school and that made me feel better. However, because I couldn't get our school district to make the proper arrangements, I would have to transport Daniel from our home in Brooklyn into the city each day—a daily commute of four hours for me by car, but still a better alternative than the train, because at five, Daniel couldn't negotiate the stairs.

After a few weeks, my phone calls continued to prove to be a waste of time and I finally decided to physically go to our district for the necessary paperwork for transportation. After an hour of stalling me, the assistant chairman replied with a big smile on his face that it was "easier said than done" to get busing services in order. He said we could deal with it at our hearing. And then he said, "Let's do lunch sometime," and winked. My stomach was churning.

I called Regina, and learned that, indeed, we were going to have to go to a hearing. By mid-October, I was still transporting Daniel back and forth to school each day. At our second impartial hearing, an enraged hearing officer listened to the district's position that it would be "very hard pressed" to provide us transportation to school because it wasn't the school of their choice. *But they had offered no choices!* And, as for Daniel's in-school approved therapies, the district maintained it wouldn't pay for the therapies on-site. Instead, we were expected to bring Daniel after school to a local public school for his therapies. At this point, Daniel wasn't even five years old. He left the house at 7:30 a.m. and got home around 4:00 pm. That suggestion was unacceptable. Irate, but compassionate toward us, the hearing officer ruled that it was illegal for the Board of Education to deny Daniel a bus and his therapeutic services. Additionally, she ordered that, effective immediately, we were entitled to have Daniel travel by car service to school, and we would be reimbursed until the district arranged for transportation. She further ordered that the district would contract with an agency to provide speech therapy, occupational therapy, and physical therapy on-site at Daniel's school. Finally, by early November, Daniel was on a bus and getting his services at school.

On the day before our third impartial hearing was scheduled—this one for tuition reimbursement—the Board of Education made an offer of settlement: Daniel's full tuition, transportation, and services would be paid for by the Board of Education. There was no need for further litigation—Daniel's *kindergarten* education was set. I couldn't imagine securing the next twelve years of schooling.

CHAPTER SIX

Summertime Oz

S ummit Camp was the summertime Oz—a magical place where magical
people turned the ordinary into the extra-ordinary, where momentarily
at least, the courage-less or lost kids for whom "mainstream camp" wasn't an
option could gain the confidence to transcend.

When Double D (as Daniel was affectionately known at Summit) stepped
off that camp bus, I knew he was transported to a world where the best of who
he was, was celebrated every day. It was a place where I had to relinquish him
for I couldn't share this part of his life, as much as I wanted to. It was his sacred
place, the place he knew was his. It was one of the hardest things I did and one
of the best things I did. Sending my son to sleep-away camp taught him to be
on his own.

The first time I took him to camp, it felt like an endless journey down the
dirt path to his bunk, a thousand questions firing from Daniel's mouth.

"What time do we eat? Do we get pizza? When do I have to go to bed?
How often do I have to go in the pool? When do we go on the trips?" His unit
leader, Mark, was patiently trying to keep up with the answers. I listened, but

could only imagine nighttime falling and my nine- year-old son lying in the dark, crying his eyes out for me—a mother's worst fear. I had to be strong. The counselor winked at me and with that gorgeous grin and British accent said, "Don't wurry, Mum, D will be just fine." After we got to his bunk and dropped off his stuff and chose his bed, Daniel said, "You can go." I was dumbfounded. I was shocked. I wanted more drama. I walked out of the bunk and knew not to look back. I went. Slowly. It took every last ounce of strength for me to keep walking. I knew it was the best thing for Daniel and it was my idea that he go to camp, but really, was he ready for this? Of course. I was the one who wasn't ready for this! I told myself my son would be well cared for, and someone would make sure he would eat the food he would surely hate, make sure his hands were cleaned every once in a while, make sure his hair was washed at least once, make sure he occasionally brushed his teeth, make sure he had clean underwear, and make sure he had the daily schedule down. I told myself that someone would understand and answer his relentless questions. I knew someone would watch that he didn't fall too far behind and get lost on a field trip, that his glasses and hearing aids were where they needed to be, and that he took his allergy medicine. I knew someone would hear him and hug him if he cried. We hoped he would feel safe and protected and loved and that he would make friends and grow. All this was really a lot to ask—considering he was going for only ten days.

I counted the hours that first summer till I would once again have the warmth of Daniel's smiles to light my days and the sweetness of his kisses and hugs to end my nights, but I had to give him the magic of sleep-away camp—I wanted my son to have that. I wanted to teach him how to be on his own. I knew I missed him far more than he missed me.

Each year thereafter when I would leave him at the bus, I was left with the token departure directions he would inimitably deliver. "DON'T EMBARRASS ME!" Or, "I hope I meet some hot girls." After he had his Bar Mitzvah, I guess he took that "manhood thing" pretty seriously. It was the year he has passed the threshold from Pokémon to girls. He demanded female "advice" from me about how to meet hot girls. I told him I couldn't really be of help in that department.

"Speak with your counselors," I said as I remembered fondly Billy Kaplan and my first kiss, snuck by surprise in an abandoned shack at my sleep-away camp.

So, by the last year he went to camp, we were at the Marriott at LaGuardia airport waiting for the bus. I was bit a more cavalier. I read the newspaper and glanced up every once in a while, watching as Double D worked the room with his old friends and counselors. That was the year his step into "manhood" included taking a newcomer, Morris, under his wing and telling him, "I will be the best big brother you ever had." Most parents dream to glimpse their children outgrowing their narcissism and reaching out to help others. I got to see it.

That first week of camp was always strange. No one to negotiate with, no one to watch movies with, no one to eat pizza and ice cream three nights a week with, no one to say "no" to, no one to solve the world's problems with, and no one's glasses to clean. This house is not home without Daniel in it. The doormen ask for him, the bagel guys ask for him, the super asks for him—the mailman, the New York City transit bus drivers all ask for him. When I would spy him on the camp Web site, I wondered why he wasn't wearing his sunglasses. Why does he not wear his hat? Are those nails clipped? Is his hair washed? Those sneakers must stink. Did he even once brush his teeth? I would try not to be a pain, so I kept the calls to the office at a minimum. And then usually by the second week, I would see one photo of him, absolutely beaming, usually on stage, and my heart would find its resting place. I would forget about the nails, and the hat, and the glasses, and the stinky sneakers. And I would know he was happy.

That last year at Summit, Daniel had been wishing and hoping he would make it onto the Banana Boat. I had been saying for four years, "You know what you have to do." Daniel was sure passing the obligatory swimming test would kill him, which is exactly what I thought, too, and why I didn't learn to swim until I was nearly an adult.

He did manage to pass the swimming test that year. Two counselors held his feet up so he couldn't walk across the pool, and for fully two laps his hands did the work—someone very nice let him pass—and he got onto that Banana Boat. He later reported to me that as soon as the boat lurched forward, he was thrown off, and he proudly recounted how he almost died. He still can't swim.

Daniel never won the award for the neatest, the most organized, the most athletic. He wasn't the best at jewelry making or woodworking, and he had a million excuses for all those things he didn't want to do. However, I was quite sure he could win an award for the camper with the most tenacity, courage, determination, generosity, and best attitude. And, I am sure the memories he made each year at camp were as good as any award he ever won.

CHAPTER SEVEN

9.11

September 12, 2001.

I breathed in Daniel's sweet scent. Outside, the air was thick with the smell of the fire that still burned in the sky. My heart cried in silence, long after the tears left my face. I smiled at Daniel. I told him I loved him. He asked if I would sing to him. I heard myself singing—that's what I did when I needed to comfort him. I closed my eyes.

In my office that horrible morning the day before, we watched the TV as the first plane crashed and tore through the Trade Center. Then the second plane hit and there was another explosion. We watched in horror as the edifice crumbled. There was a mess of rubble and twisted metal and broken glass and the gray smoke and dust that hung over everything. There were the images playing over and over again in my mind, the crashing and people running, and those souls who met their salvation mid-air in their last attempt to escape the inferno. What does one think of as they free fall from one hundred stories? I can't imagine. How many lives have been lost? How many survivors? Waves of disbelief and grief washed over me. I had to make sure everyone in the office was okay. I had to make sure those who had family members who worked in the Trade Center were okay to leave. There was a lot of crying and hugging. I had to get everyone out of the office. The screams of the people on the streets below beckoned me to Daniel. I had to get to my son.

When I got downstairs, people were running and looking up the block at the Met Life building towering above us. They were screaming that it was next. I began running in the other direction toward Fifth Avenue. As I ran, I just kept thinking that I might never see my son again. I ran. No one was talking, just running and looking back. I am no runner. It got harder to breathe. There were names flying through my head—I heard myself saying them out loud. All those people I loved. Why didn't those three guys I left in the office leave right away? *I told them to leave.* What were they thinking? Someone grabbed my arm. A stranger. She said everything was going to be okay. I held onto her. She must have heard me talking out loud. I was shaking. I had to get to Daniel. I told myself to slow down. My heart felt like it would explode. I didn't even know where Alan was. We were divorced already for two years. I wasn't even sure if he was in the country. Past St. Patrick's Cathedral, past the GM building— each, one less target. Past Central Park, no one would bomb us up here, right? I looked to the sky, to the north it was blue, and to the south it was black.

When I arrived home, my boyfriend Peter was waiting for me. He had the plan. Get the car. If we can't get the car, get to Queens. Rent a car. Take stuff. How much stuff? We might not have been coming home. A change of clothes for Daniel, Daniel's Kermit toy, water. The walls were closing behind us. The city was shutting down.

"Let's go," Peter said. "We *have* to go." His voice was too controlled and too quiet.

We both wiped tears from our faces. We were okay. We were together. Daniel was okay. He was at school on Long Island. We walked out to York Avenue. I had already half-walked, half-run fifty or sixty blocks in my heels. My feet were blistered and bleeding but I didn't care. I had to get to my son at school. I learned later they told the children that the parents who could make it were coming, that there was a bad accident and a lot of traffic. At the time, however, I knew little. Using a cell phone was impossible; the circuits were all busy.

We walked the forty-five blocks back to mid-town to the garage by the United Nations. I kept telling Peter on the way down, "they won't let us take the car—the whole area by the UN is under surveillance." It seemed odd to me, but they let us take the car out. They should have denied us entry and exit to the garage. They should have, but they didn't.

"That was strange," I said as we drove out onto First Avenue.

"No," Peter said. "No, it wasn't. I know you. You would have walked to get to your son; this way it's easier." He reached for my hand.

We drove around to the entrance to the Midtown Tunnel. It was a fortress of police cars. We pulled up to one of them. I looked at the officer. We both had sunglasses on. He looked past the dark lenses into my eyes. Did he see the desperate fear? Did he hear me say, "Please, please, let us get through the tunnel; I have to get to my son! He is only nine. He is a child with special needs. He will be afraid. Please." No, he didn't hear me, because I thought it, but never said a word. He looked at me a few seconds, and then waved us on. With a flick of his wrist, we were free to go. There was no one in front of us and as I turned to look back, no one behind us. Why us? Why? Why had he let us go? I had never seen the Midtown Tunnel empty. The Long Island Expressway was empty, too. On the other side, the cars were backed up for miles. The tunnel in both directions was closed.

My mind raced back to a time when Daniel was three. He was in the back seat of the car. I was driving. I was taking him to his doctor in Manhattan because I hated the emergency room in our Brooklyn neighborhood. I could hear him gasping for air. It seemed like he would stop breathing any minute. His face was grayish blue. There was so much traffic. We were downtown and we had to make it uptown to Eighty-third Street to his pediatrician's office. He had a bad cough and now it seemed his throat was closing up. I was terrified. I kept talking to him. I talked to him the way I did when I was only six weeks pregnant and we were rushing across the Brooklyn Bridge. I was talking to him telling him, "It's okay, it's okay. Keep breathing, sweetie." But I thought he was going to die. I should have taken him to the local hospital. At least they wouldn't have let him die. I scanned every corner for a cop. Where were they when you needed one? I told myself to keep driving. I thought about stopping at Beth Israel's emergency room, but I kept going. I wanted our doctor. She would know what to do. She was a pulmonary specialist. There were so many cars in front of me and they were not moving. I was shaking. I had only been a mother for a short time; my son was so little, and I felt so helpless.

When we got to the doctor's office, strangely there was no one there. I carried Daniel's limp body into the reception area. I screamed out, "Hello! Hello!" There was no one. Finally, a nurse came from the back; she was wiping food from her face. I could barely speak. "I... I... He's not breathing." We put him down on an examining table. She'd know what to do. She'd know... She left for a minute and came back with an oxygen mask for him, and placed it over his face. She began to check his oxygen saturation levels. It felt like hours, but maybe it was only minutes. One of the doctors in the practice came in, and apologized for not being there. I didn't care why they weren't there. I didn't hear her. They were just words. We talked about getting an ambulance.... Daniel was breathing a little better. I explained that I thought his throat was closing up. Another doctor came in. My sweater was soaked with sweat. I heard someone calling over to the emergency room at Mount Sinai. I heard them saying my name, that I was coming in with my son. I scooped him up from the table and ran outside for a cab. No ambulance; I could get a cab faster. "Keep breathing, sweetie," I said. "Keep breathing."

X-rays, emergency room, oxygen, nice young doctor. I always liked those curtains that swish so fast, metal on metal. Swishing open, swishing closed. I lay on the bed with my son in my arms. The doctors didn't have a reason. Maybe croup, but no, his throat wasn't closing. They gave him steroids through an inhalation system. We rested. Hours later, as I left with him, Daniel was smiling and asking the doctor questions. Questions. Daniel was always asking questions. When the questions started, I knew he would be fine. Children come running back from death's doorway. I limped out of there with him. I was exhausted. We went back to the doctor's office. She recommended we stay a little while to monitor him, and we were ushered into an examining room. She set me up with a mask for Daniel. He did not like it, but I curled up next to him, and wrapped my arms around him. As I held the mask over his face, we fell asleep.

But now it was six years later. Daniel was nine and I felt the same over-powering need to be with him. As Peter and I approached the school in Glen Cove, I felt my heart start beating faster. I wanted to run from the car and grab Daniel and just hold him and smell him and tell him how much I loved him. Outside his classroom, my knees buckled. I knelt on the floor and wept. His teacher came out and told me I had to pull myself together, that my son couldn't see me this way. I wiped my nose and eyes, and put my sunglasses back on and walked into the room. He was in his favorite chair, reading. I stood behind him, and watched him for a minute. He looked up and said in that sing songy little voice, "Oh hi, Mommy. Hi, Peter." I took him in my arms and held him there as if I would never let go, till he wrenched away from me. We went to T.G.I.Friday's and sat there watching CNN as the planes flew into the buildings over and over again. I tried to block Daniel's view of the TV, but he saw what was going on. We couldn't drive back to the city. The tunnels and bridges were closed. We would have to keep driving east. I got the yellow pages and searched for a hotel. No luck. I called a client who had a home in The Hamptons, who agreed to let us stay there. We had no idea how long we'd be there. But we were safe and we were together. But for how long we didn't know.

That night I lay next to my son, I reached for his hand, and answered his questions. "What happened? Why couldn't we go home? Why did a plane fly into a building? Who would do this? Why? Did people die? How many people died?" Mostly, I said, "I don't know, honey. I wish I could tell you, I just don't know." He drifted off to sleep in my arms. I listened to his slow, even breathing. In the listening there was peace. I crawled into bed next to Peter. We clung to each other and cried again.

The next morning, we didn't say much. We were thinking it but we never said it to each other, "Was it a dream? Is it over?" Two weeks earlier, we had emerged from the Fulton Street subway stop. We turned and looked back. I pointed and said to my niece, Ashley, and to Daniel, "Stop, guys, Look! There are the Twin Towers. They are almost the tallest buildings in the world, and that is where some of the world's most powerful businesses are." We stood in that spot for what was just a few seconds, just looking down the block.

On the next day, the day after the Twin Towers fell, we weren't sure what to do. We went to a golf driving range. It was the most normal thing we could do. Peter played nine holes of golf. Daniel and I banged away at some golf balls. We kept checking in the pro shop for the news. By 5:00 p.m., one of the bridges and the Midtown Tunnel were reopened.

As we drove toward the tunnel, I saw the black smoke rising and the hole in the skyline. Daniel was chattering away in the back seat. He had lost a tooth. There was a hole in his mouth where it once was. A small loss—a new tooth would grow in its place. As we drove, we wrote a letter to the tooth fairy. I was trying to think of happy things. Daniel's friend, Michael turned eleven—a celebration. We were alive. Ahead of us, there was a hole in the sky and nothing, nothing would ever be the same. When we got home I searched for an old photo. My best friend and I were twenty. We skipped class that day. We went to the top of World Trade Center. We ate grapes and talked about all the things we were going to do with our lives. She called from Northern California to make sure we were okay. There were no towers anymore. The sky was empty there. The world was fractured, in how many places I couldn't imagine. I thought about the arrivals and departures, the knowns and the unknowns that had forever changed me since the day Kathleena and I had taken that picture—marriage, birth, death, divorce, and the day that would come to be known as 9/11. Later, I thought of the letting go, the letting go, of how we must let go, and how hard it is, but that is the only way peace comes.

Daniel slept peacefully. I closed my eyes and thought of how I had told him the angels would come and bring him sweet dreams. I thought of the cop. I thought maybe he heard my sister, Amy, whispering to him from heaven, telling him to let us drive through that tunnel. I lay in bed and clung to my pillow. I couldn't let go of the promise I had made to Daniel that the tooth fairy would still come.

CHAPTER EIGHT

And Now, You Are a Man

I couldn't sleep. Daniel's Bar Mitzvah weekend was a whirlwind of moments I was savoring. I closed my eyes. I was dancing and laughing with Daniel until we lost our breath. My face hurt from smiling so much. My eyes were burning from the mascara that ran into my eyes all day. I was sure my sister, Amy, who had passed on when Daniel was three, had witnessed the miracle from her place in heaven.

The night before, when we were in our hotel room in Falmouth, Massachusetts, Daniel was so nervous, and for the first time said he wasn't sure he could do it. I gently reminded him of the time when he didn't think he'd like sleep-away camp or a new school, how he handled a kid who had bullied him, how he thought he'd hate a certain food he had never tasted, how he thought he'd never wear his hearing aids. All those things had worked out.

"Open your palm," I said. He did so.

I placed an imaginary handful of something in it and tucked his fingers closed.

"Now, open your palm again," I said. "Remember you have my heart right there, and that my love for you is always there when you want it.

"When you stand on the bimah, and you close your eyes, you think of what you have in your hand, okay? And remember, you love to be on stage, right? This is YOUR show!"

I gave him a big hug, and I leaned over and blew the worries from his head.

That day we went to the synagogue was cold and gray for May, but it was New England and it did not concern me. It was still a beautiful day. I looked around; there were 125 friends and family members who had traveled from New York and all over the country to be there—talking, smiling, rustling programs. The sounds bounced around and got lost in the high ceiling. Daniel sat on the bimah. He looked younger than his thirteen years, but I had never seen him look so grown up. He was perched in the large chair that looked like a throne, in the navy suit and red tie he picked out. He was surveying all of us, nodding, and smiling, holding court. No matter how dressed up he was, or how carefully he had been prepared, I saw beyond his composure. He was nervous. I caught his eye. He cocked his head and gave me one of his quirky smiles and then he looked down and away. I held up a tight fist to remind him. He wasn't fidgeting as much as I thought he might. He looked down at his prayer book.

The memories of the first time he took a step toward me and the first page he read—both long-awaited and hard-won triumphs—were now separated by the years that have passed and the rows of people between us. I felt so far from him and yet so close. Today, my son would emerge from boyhood to declare himself a young man.

Rabbi Elias began playing his guitar softly. Daniel stepped forward. The only sounds in the temple were the notes of the guitar and the chanting that Rabbi Elias began. I looked back and caught the eye of Regina, out attorney, who had known Daniel since he was three. We just nodded to each other, our eyes tearing. There wasn't anything to say. We were there. My son made it to this day. That was all we needed to know.

I looked up at the stained glass windows and the gray light that illuminated the biblical depiction of Abraham and Isaac on the mountain. God tested Abraham, asking him to sacrifice his son. The story challenges every last bit of strength and consciousness I had. How? How could God demand this of a man who loved his son? I will never understand the story no matter how many times it is sermonized or explained. How could I have carried my son up a mountain and offered him as a sacrifice? My son fills my every second with life. How, how would I do this? The story has often defied me. And yet, Abraham, who couldn't have understood God's intention, trusted so deeply that he humbly followed the command. As hard as it was, despite the unknown, he was led by his faith up that mountain.

The Rabbi coaxed every voice to fill the synagogue with chanting. I closed my eyes and listened to the sound of 150 congregants. I counted among my blessings this gathering of my given and chosen family and my many friends, from New York, California, Texas, Virginia, Chicago, and Florida. Even Peter's parents from The Netherlands had come so far to be with us.

When Daniel turned twelve, I had explained to him that a Jewish boy *becomes* a Bar Mitzvah; it wasn't something he would *do*. At twelve, in the Jewish faith, he was designated a responsible member of society. His actions would no longer be protected by his parents, and from that point forth he would stand of his own accord. He would be made accountable. Accountability is a serious word for any young boy in today's world, especially one whose independence hung precariously in the unknown. My son's independence was the most cherished hope I could have for him.

When a Jewish boy celebrates his becoming a Bar Mitzvah, he traditionally leads the Saturday morning Sabbath service. It could take years of study to read from the Torah, which is the highest honor. Daniel had been attending small special education private schools since he was three. Despite predictions to the contrary, he could read English quite well, but I wasn't sure how we would handle the Hebrew as he had not been to Hebrew school. I knew of children who had been privately tutored. Daniel had seemed mildly interested, but said he had to "think about it," which I thought was fair. I had attended five years of Hebrew school—my traditional, conservative Jewish upbringing left me no choice—but my Bat Mitzvah was one of the most memorable days of my life and I had hoped my son would take me up on my offer. The idea of being privately tutored in preparation for this seemed like a lot of work and wasn't very appealing to my son, but the promise of a nice party bettered the offer. Lisa, the radiant and beautiful young Rabbi who made the private lessons seem very, very attractive, closed the deal.

As I contemplated the service and the traditional party, it occurred to me that more than the spectacle, I wanted to preserve the integrity of the day. Daniel and I had attended services in New York City only a few times, and it felt to me that we needed to be somewhere more nurturing and familiar. Being from New England, I approached my mother, thinking that perhaps her synagogue where she and my father were quite active would be a solution. Rabbi Elias was exceptionally gracious and welcoming. As long-distance members, we were not the typical congregants. We met with Rabbi Elias over the year, and those meetings involved mostly poignant discussions, wherein the Rabbi and Daniel would briefly talk and Daniel would ask an avalanche of questions and Rabbi Elias would patiently answer.

For a complex child with learning issues, the Bar Mitzvah day takes on another meaning. It is also a triumph of belonging, of doing what others do, of not being different. The other complication for Daniel was that Alan and I had been divorced since he was eight and the family dynamics had been somewhat stressed. It was a privilege for me to plan this day, but I saw it as even more personal because I was solely responsible for the planning and execution of everything. It was also one of the few times as a parent I was having an experience both as a mother and as a Jew planning a rite of passage that did not exclude my son.

After Daniel gave me his final commitment, I didn't interfere. I never once tested him. I trusted that if he said he would do it, he would do it. Lisa, Daniel's Rabbi/tutor, would come, and Daniel seemed happy enough to see her—probably because she was warm, giving, and beautiful, but I trusted Daniel and that it would all work out. Rabbi Elias prepared materials and CDs for Daniel to study. Along with the study of Daniel's Torah portion, Lisa taught Daniel what it means to be Jewish. As the weeks progressed, Daniel was becoming more and more interested and getting excited.

A few minutes after the service began, Daniel's father and I were called up to the bimah to wrap Daniel in his tallis—the same tallis that we had been wrapped in when we were married. It was the first time Alan and I had stood together in six years. Despite the issues we had, that tallis symbolized for me the union that brought this child into my life, the gift of strength we could give him and the promise that we would always, always love him.

The Rabbi called my name. As I ascended the stairs I thought, "This is why I was put here on this planet—to stand by my son's side. I brought him with me through the fog and fear of the unknown, and we went up Everest. Whatever tests await us, we are ready. We are here on earth together."

The service went on for almost three hours. Daniel remained self-assured the whole time. Every once in a while when our eyes would lock; he would smile and look away. As the service neared its end, I was called forward to deliver my speech.

"My Dear Daniel." I heard my voice cut through the stillness. I looked over at my son. I touched his hand. He looked tired. Of course he was tired, it had been a long morning, but he had done it. I was so proud.

I knew you long before I saw you. I knew I would one day have one son, and that you would make every sunrise and sunset more glorious, and though I didn't know your name, now that I know you, it is the only name I could ever imagine for you—Daniel which means, "with God as my judge."

I believe I was called into your life and you into mine. When we set out on this journey, there was so much about life and love and myself I had to learn, and you have been my guide. The road has not always been easy but we have traveled far from your first fragile moments to this amazing day. On the day you came into this world, I dreamed you would be a very special child. I dream now that you will be a special person all your life—not because you were born special, but because you choose to be special.

I didn't realize how hard it would be that first time I left you after you were born, or how I would cry when I put you on the school bus. I can still see your hand leaving mine, that first time I let go when we crossed the street. I never could have known how I would feel the first time you spoke a word, took your first steps, or read a sentence from a book—maybe those things were all harder for you than other kids, but your determination peeled my heart open like a flower, and for me those moments will last forever.

It is easy for me to say "I love you." But I love who you have become. I love your inimitable and unique sense of humor. I love that your favorite two historical figures are Abraham Lincoln and Martin Luther King. I love that you are always the one who reaches out to help others, the one who offers an encouraging word, the one who tries to bridge a gap. You will look for the sunshine on the cloudiest day. You are always the one who will give of yourself so someone else can benefit. You will negotiate the "yes" out of every "no."

I have longed for answers about the world I brought you into. I wish I could make it a more peaceful place for you, but I can only try to teach you how to find peace in your heart. I can only teach you that tolerance is not enough. I pray the world you live in won't be threatened by differences, and that you will be exemplary in embracing diversity.

I can only teach you to know that your abilities are gifts, and every challenge is an opportunity. I can only teach you never to lose your curiosity and to keep an open mind. You are privileged to live as you do, in this country, in these times, surrounded by your family and friends who love you.

The tallis you wear today is a symbol of courage. I don't know anyone braver than you. The yarmulke you have upon your head is a symbol that there is a great power in the universe to guide you. The flames of the Sabbath candles will shine so that you will know on the other side of darkness there is light, and greatness can be born of adversity. When you were four, you were enrolled in a music class. You were learning about various cultures. Your teacher had asked that each child walk along some cardboard blocks that symbolized the Great Wall of China. Two or three children quickly pranced upon the blocks and within seconds, ran to the end. When it was your turn, you stepped up on the first block, steadied yourself, took three steps and fell. You tried to balance yourself, but you fell again. Quickly, you got up, moved the blocks back into place and stepped back up. I held my breath and in the silence, I heard your little voice saying "I can do this. I can do this." You were the only child who couldn't run, but you cared so much about making it to the end of that "great wall," and you were smiling the whole way.

Whenever you need to steady yourself, remember that voice that tells you, "I can do this," because you can. And know, yours has been the voice I have heard when at times I didn't know how I would put one foot in front of the other. May you find your footing to dance your way through life, Daniel, and I will be dancing right there in your heart every step of the way.

At first I thought he was very tired—he was rubbing his eyes, and his head was down—and then Daniel threw his arms round my neck and broke down. He held onto me as if he would never let go. I looked through my tears at his head, buried in my chest. I was riveted in that spot, holding my son. When I finally stepped away, I didn't look back.

Early on, when we were first given his Torah portion, I wasn't sure how I felt when I read the words from Leviticus in which the laws of who shall and shall not serve God are clearly articulated with specific references to "defective, maimed and imperfect" people being unfit to serve in the temple. When I first read the English translation of his assigned portion, I thought I must challenge it. How could I let my son recite a Bar Mitzvah portion that directly stated anyone with a physical handicap couldn't serve God? I am a rebel. But the Torah is read one passage for each day; those passages can't be chronologically rearranged or chosen to fit the "mood" of the day. It was very disturbing. I am his mother. I had to protect him from this, I thought. This is his Bar Mitzvah. There is nothing joyful about this. But no, no, I couldn't protect him from this. I couldn't protect him from so much of life. And so I let it be. Daniel and I never discussed it.

Later that night, we were lying in bed talking.

He said, "By the way, about your speech today, it was very overwhelming."

"I know," I said. "It was overwhelming for me, too. Sometimes that feeling of being so overwhelmed is a good thing; it makes us know how alive we are.

What about your Torah portion?" I asked. "We never really discussed it. What did you think of what is said?"

"Yeah, that was so unfair that people like me who have handwriting disabilities and other problems, couldn't have been priests. That is really not right, but you know that was a long time ago and we had to get over it. There are more important things to focus on nowadays."

"Do you know I am so proud of you?"

"Yeah, I know," he said. And he closed his eyes. I kissed his head and remembered that someone once told me there are no miracles, only miraculous people.

I whispered to him, "Daniel, *you* are miraculous." I am not sure he heard me. And I watched him fall asleep.

CHAPTER NINE

Saks

I pulled back on the heavy glass door and stepped out of the July heat. I could feel a rush of cold air blow across my bare arms. My high heels clicking kept the rhythm of my fast walk. Cosmetics reps were hawking. The sounds of hustling, scurrying, consuming swirled up from the floor. Hundreds of perfumes blending together wafted at me. I heard the dinging of the elevators, and saw shoppers from all over the world moving quickly, on a mission. I looked like I belonged here in Saks, but I didn't feel like I had much in common with anyone I saw. My genetically well-engineered body moved gracefully and at my command. If success has a look, perhaps it began for me when, at three years old, I insisted on choosing my own wardrobe, but this well-crafted appearance is not the whole story.

I moved past jewelry and handbags, while Daniel, fourteen, dragged his feet. It would be a rare sight if he were walking by my side. It would be an even rarer sight if his pants were pulled up, and their bottoms were not shredded from being stepped on. His glasses were not clean, as usual, and had slipped down to their usual resting place on his freckled nose. His thick dark hair is always tufted and no matter who cuts it, it always looks a little unkempt. He was a little chubby with a slight dark shadow emerging on his upper lip, the heralding signs of impending adolescence, and I wondered what it would be like to teach him how to shave. I wondered what he was thinking as I whisked along and he shuffled behind me. I sometimes wonder what people see, too, when they look at us.

When I began my departure from the mainstream, I didn't go kicking or screaming; I don't remember sadness. I remember the fight for a threatened pregnancy and love. Just love. I stand up and sit up straight and move with the practiced grace of a dancer or gymnast; he ambles along. I walk the streets in a meditative silence. He trails behind me observing every detail of street life, while rattling off endless questions.

"Why are the sirens so loud? Why is this man in front of us walking so slowly? Why is it so cold out? How much further do we have to walk? Let's take a cab...."

I listened and answered: "I don't know why the sirens are so loud. I don't know why that man is so slow. Why are *you* so slow? We have to walk until we get where we are going. No, we're not taking a cab. I didn't notice that. Hmmm, why do you think it's so cold?"

I don't suffer that same need-to-know-everything-about-everything-every-second. I suffer the kind of middle-aged minutia and insecurities that make plastic surgeons rich and the enormity of raising my child single-handedly while running a business. My hobby is trying to look good while I do it. That is why we were in Saks.

As I made my way to the MAC counter to buy a lipstick that day, Daniel was rattling off questions again:

"What time are we going to be home?"

"Why?" I asked.

"Because there's a show I want to watch."

"Well, I'm not sure."

"Well, what time do you *estimate* we'll be home?"

"I don't know," I said.

"When I am President," he announced, "I will have a limousine."

He liked to talk about the "fact" that he will be President.

"Why a limousine?" I turned and asked, and realized that even with his hearing aids, all the noise made it impossible for him to hear me.

"Me too," I said. Loudly. "I always wanted a limousine—and a private plane, too."

He was still behind me.

"Why do you want a limousine so badly?"

"So I wouldn't have to walk anywhere," he said.

I long ago stopped wondering what it would be like to have a child who *could* be President, or who *would* walk faster. The fact that he walks is a gift. I once asked him if he could do anything besides be President what it would be and he said he would move the planets around.

"Move the planets around?" I queried. "And why would you move the planets around?"

"So I can get a better look at Pluto."

"Why a better look at Pluto?"

"So I would know for once and for all if it were a star or a planet."

Of course, I listened intently. I remember still the days when he could hardly speak. I wanted to hear every word he had to say. I didn't know there was any doubt as to whether Pluto was a star or a planet until recently, when there was a news report that Pluto may not be the full-fledged planet we thought it is. It is a star. I have no idea how Daniel knew; he just knew.

Daniel thought about the big picture and so did I. Daniel was overly confident of his future. He regularly talked about being President or a TV producer. I, on the other hand, despite my relative success, had no sense of how the future would unfold. I wondered how I would take care of the both of us and the dog, alone.

As we moved through the store, I noticed some women looking at us. I remembered a babysitter telling me that she got very angry when people in public places looked at Daniel for too long. I told her I appreciated that she cared so much. I usually don't notice. After we left the MAC counter, I looked back every so many steps. Daniel was still back there. This is how we have walked for years. I had heard myself say so many times, "Daniel, pick it up, c'mon, let's go." And then sometimes I slowed down and remembered how long I waited for him to take those first steps. Even when I didn't have a clue where I was headed, I wanted to get there quickly. As we left the store, I stopped by a mirror. I scrutinized my face, and checked out the new lipstick. Daniel didn't stop. He was walking in front of me. He took a right on Forty-ninth and headed for Madison. From behind him I watched his uneven gait. "Let's see how long before he looks back," I thought.

But he kept walking.

"Hey," I called to him loudly. "SLOW DOWN."

And then I thought, "Maybe today is the day I will walk slower."

Daniel turned around and smiled back at me. "Let's take a cab," he said. And he kept walking.

CHAPTER TEN

28 Boxes

Alan stood in the hallway and looked at me. He looked at the floor, and then he looked up. He said the house wasn't as he hoped it would be. He turned and slowly began walking up the stairs. I followed with Daniel. I had left on a September day in 1999 with twenty-eight boxes, and I didn't take my key. When I closed the door for the last time, it locked behind me. I had returned because a few months earlier, right after Daniel's Bar Mitzvah, Alan had been diagnosed with terminal cancer. I had not been close to Alan in all those years and had barely seen him. I asked if I could come in when I came to pick up Daniel.

We had been married for nine years. On the day I left nearly seven years earlier, it had been pouring out. I had turned back once and looked at the lintels, the black door, the edifice built in the late 1800s that had housed our life for ten years. It was substantial, with its thousands of red bricks, occupying the whole corner. Two years after we were married, I came home to find Alan had carved his initials in the new concrete outside. My initials weren't next to his. I remember feeling sad as if my missing initials were a clue that it might end.

On that rainy day in September when I left with only twenty-eight boxes, I was forty-one years old. I had no family close by to help. I wasn't financially secure. I had no plan really. I was in a lot of pain, and I had to leave. We had been negotiating our separation agreement for too long. Daniel would stay with me until Alan and I had some finalized agreement in place. I had been hearing all my life I was strong, but so was the Titanic.

Tears fell from my face and mixed with the pelting rain and ran into the gutter. I stood there and watched the movers leave with the boxes, each carefully labeled as if the Bubble Wrap could protect the good memories and the labels might justify the remnants of my broken life. Only the baby pictures and the tapes of Daniel really mattered.

My eight-year-old son didn't know it yet but I would make his new room on the Upper East Side of Manhattan a haven where even a world that was crumbling apart could feel safe—I prayed he wouldn't remember this day. I wanted him to know that when I walked down the aisle to marry his father I had dreamed of so much. How would I explain the ambivalence, the pain I felt as I became a refugee, a statistic—fleeing all that I had known for a life I would have to create? I wondered if my son would ever understand. I was heartbroken. I had returned to work just a couple of years earlier. I had no evidence that I could do this: put my life back together, succeed at a relatively new job, raise my young son, make a stable home for us. I told myself that entrepreneurs risk vast sums of money on the unknown. I would have to risk the safety of the life I knew, for the faith I had in myself. I would have to.

As I stood there on the landing, now almost seven years later, looking at Alan, I thought back over the time since I had left. I had barely seen him. I knew very little about his life, or his relationships. I had reestablished my career, I had fallen in and out of love, Daniel and I lived independently. Those years were harder than any I had known. I had landed a job at a large and very prestigious talent agency in New York. The odds of this were unlikely especially being three years out of work at the time, but my reputation had remained strong. I was very fortunate that someone thought of me for a position that was being created in a new department. I wasn't accustomed to the rigors of a nine-to-six—and sometimes later—office job and the pressures associated with a highly competitive business, while also caring for my son whose needs far exceeded those of a typical child. The additional stress of an unraveling marriage made me sometimes feel that rebuilding my life would break me. But slowly, I was able to establish a client list and substantiate a good business. After we moved, I looked for bargains and shopped for furnishings. With each piece of furniture, each glass or plate, our apartment was becoming a home. Daniel was sad at times. He didn't always want to go back and forth between his parent's homes, and Alan and I were so polarized I knew that was hard on him, but he loved school and camp. I kept encouraging him to see that life is like a stew of many emotions—like a good recipe, we strive to find the balance of those experiences.

It was unclear to me during all that time, how Alan had been doing. Daniel was very young, and I didn't want to ask too many questions. As I stood there on the landing looking at Alan, I wanted to go inside the house, maybe in the same way one stops to look at an accident—with deep curiosity and fear and hoping it will be better than one thinks. Two Sundays a month, I would leave Daniel for a week. I wouldn't look back after he entered the house. I would try not to think about it. I would turn on the steps and walk back to the car, back to my life in the city, and I would try to forget all the reasons why I had left Brooklyn.

I climbed the stairs to the world where we had been a family for a decade's worth of memories. The walls were still standing but nothing else was familiar. The floors were worn now. The walls needed paint. The door to the washing machine was open. There were clothes on the once white floor. I peered into the doorway where Alan's office had been. It looked like it had been a while since he had worked there. As I passed the second floor landing, I peeked outside. My rose bushes that had once climbed their trellis were nothing more than dead stubs. There was no hint of the snapdragons and iris that had once reached for the sky. There was only a pile of gray, broken, planks. As I walked through the space that once comforted me, the only thing familiar was the chasm that hung in the silence between Alan and me, and the years we had barely spoken. I wondered how long he had been sick.

We had met in a bar twenty years before. Behind his glasses, I thought his eyes were blue like a cloudless sky. He told me that he was an artist and a photographer. I hoped he thought I was pretty. I dragged on my cigarette and turned my head, letting a slow steady stream of smoke trickle from my lips. And when I turned back, I asked him if he minded the smoke. He hated it. I liked his honesty, or so I thought. We left the bar and went to his car. It was cold outside and the heat of our breath had fogged the windows. He placed his foot on the windshield and drew a fish from the shape it left. He made me laugh.

Enough good times and men led me to realize then, at thirty, it was time to settle down. I married Alan, ten years my senior. It seemed like it was a good balance. Between us we had a lot of friends, we liked enough of the same things, we traveled, we both liked good food and red wines, and we both learned how to scuba dive, which became a passion. I thought when I took my wedding vows I knew who I was and who I was marrying—we both felt like together we equaled more than one-plus-one—but I discovered I had no idea who he and I were becoming. I know now the mortar is not material wealth or common interests or goals; it is not even love, because love can be based on desires, wants, and needs. The mortar in a marriage is the way two people find each other and who they become together day by day in the face of prosperity and adversity. The mortar is the looking into each other and at each other and looking outward and discovering what they both see while looking in the same direction.

After Daniel was born, my commitment to my son rivaled everything else in my life. My career could be re-forged. However, marriage is a tale told through the delicate balance of love and need and expectation. I held on as long as I could; we tried to work on it, but our definition of partnership differed. The dynamics between us eventually left me feeling depleted, exhausted, and unfulfilled. My only hope upon leaving was that one day Alan and I would become friends and that we would find a way to keep our son's best interests in the foreground of whatever transpired between us.

When I turned the key to unlock the door of our new apartment in the city, there was so much I didn't know about myself. Daniel didn't ask for this new life. He had plenty of his own issues already and I recognized that my son was going to suffer through the loss of his family as he knew it. Over the following years, I would discover I had to trust my intuition. I had to develop a willingness to see that there was no settlement or money that could right whatever blame, resentment, broken promises, and anger I had. My son most needed me to be present, to show up in the moment. Now that I was alone, I had to find out what I wanted and to accept the truth that my life wasn't what I had planned. I learned to listen to my son and to pay attention. And though I was challenged with feelings of loss and failure, in mothering Daniel I discovered I wasn't as lost as I sometimes felt.

As I entered the kitchen in Brooklyn, I realized it was my love for my son that brought me there. I came in the spirit of forgiveness. I didn't want to be hurt or angry anymore.

I looked down. There on the living room floor, in the piles of papers and magazines, I remembered the small, curly-haired nymph-like child who took out all his books and left them all over the floor. Daniel was three then. He loved singing along with Raffi, "He's got the whole world, in his hands..."

I walked into the master bedroom. Alan hadn't wanted to buy the white Berber that was still in the room. Once, Daniel had stood right there by the TV and made a BM on the floor. I stood on that spot. I looked at the fireplace. Years ago when Alan brought home those handmade glass doors, he said, "Look at these doors! They are like jewelry; you cannot just go out and buy these." They were now hidden behind a large plasma TV that sat propped on a chair, wires trailing from its backside.

As I moved through the house, Alan and I barely made eye contact. I knew he had recently undergone radiation and chemotherapy. Grief and uncertainty hung everywhere like the cotton cobwebs one hangs for Halloween. No one said a word. In the stillness of that afternoon, in the bedroom that had been ours, I felt I was standing in the outward manifestation of how our lives had changed. I wanted to cry. I knew there was a finality to this diagnosis. I knew because I watched my sister die of a terminal disease and I wanted to reach out, to hug Alan. I looked at Daniel, now fourteen. When last I saw him in his room here, he was eight. He looked so big. I tried to imagine my son's life, and what it was like for him, living between our two homes. This was the house where he was born, but not the life I dreamed of for him. I wanted to tell him about his first birthday party, the hundred balloons that bobbed around and scared him when they popped, the clown cream birthday cake that he dug his fingers into, and the bears that danced on strings above him as he slept. The things that I had left in his room were still there, a baby picture, a music box, some books he had when he was very small. These were the only signs that I had ever been a part of this home. I heard the birds outside. They were still there. I just stood there in the doorway. Daniel came up beside me and took my hand.

"Mom."

I said nothing. He must have been watching me.

"Mom, it's okay."

"Of course it is." I whispered.

I turned around, wiped my hands on my pants, and swallowed. We would go back to the smell of cookies we could bake. We would go home and make dinner and listen to music and hang out with our dog Gracie. I thought about the words I had said to his father sixteen years earlier, "Till death do us part."

"Can we get ice cream on the way home?" Daniel asked.

"Of course we can."

I didn't know how I would shepherd Daniel through his father's illness, how my son, who had required so much care, would grow up and take care of his own father. I wanted to protect him from all of this, but I had to trust he was emerging from boyhood to become the young man he was meant to be.

Alan battled his cancer for years after that. His daily challenges were compounded by his having few friends and no one close to him nearby. Daniel dutifully visited each week; we both offered help in whatever way we could. After watching years of his father's chemotherapy, hospitalizations, and declining health, Daniel asked, "Do you help my father because you love him?"

I waited a few seconds before I answered, "I have tried to be a good friend, sweetheart. I find ways to be loving. I try to honor the history and the unique person your father is. I try to help in whatever way I can. You know, the important thing is that you know your father loves you very much.

"Love is complicated," he said.

"Yes, it is…. Yes, it is."

CHAPTER ELEVEN

Picture Day

"Picture Day" started at 6:30 a.m. with the merciless beeping of my alarm clock. I despise the alarm clock. I despise morning in general. I despise late fall mornings because of the cold and the darkness. I rolled over. Gracie, our dog, was lying on my head and her bad breath was enough to drive me from my bed. I groped my way to the kitchen where I realized I had forgotten to set the coffee on "automatic" and that my bare feet were cold on the tiles because my slippers were back in my room. In one of my fantasies, there would be someone else to make the coffee and there'd be someone to call out to fetch my slippers too. BUT, no, I reminded myself, I was alone by *choice*. I was the one who broke up with my boyfriend. There's no one to fetch my slippers, no one to cuddle with, and no one to make the coffee but me

Daniel sleeps so deeply that waking him up is like resurrecting him from the dead. I stepped closer to his bed. My foot landed in something warm and wet.

"What the hell!" I hissed.

My son didn't flinch. In the corner, Princess Gracie sat cowering.

"WHAT DID YOU DO?" I glared at her as if she could answer.

Still no movement from Daniel. I ran for paper towels, and then I banished Gracie to her bed and pointed at her not to move. I yanked the covers off Daniel.

He slowly rolled over and mumbled, "It's Picture Day."

"Daniel, you'll miss your bus. I have to run Gracie out; she just made a mess in the house. I have no time. PLEASE, GET UP and get dressed!"

"But Mom, it is Picture Day. Where are my GOOD clothes?"

"Good clothes? I don't know. You don't even like good clothes. Daniel, it's pouring. C'mon, hurry up."

I stepped out into the torrential rain, dog in arms, feeling about as much enthusiasm as I had, stepping in her poop. We only had her for two weeks and this was the first rain. She refused to walk. I dragged her up and down the sidewalk. No poop. No pee. I grabbed the wet, shivering thing, tucked her under arm, and carried her back upstairs. There wasn't anything more pathetic than how she looked when I saw her mug shot from the adoption agency online, and so this homeless waif had become an Upper East Side princess. I was sure she had pooped and peed outside when she was wandering on the streets. At that moment, Princess Gracie was making me question my sanity.

As I stepped into the house, I heard Daniel calling to me, as if he had no idea I had gone out.

"Daniel, I can't hear you when you call to me from another room." His hearing aids were probably still on his desk and he probably didn't even hear me.

As I walked into the kitchen, he said, "Can you make me my lunch?"

Lunch. I thought, "Oh NO. I am not making you your lunch. Buy your lunch. Skip lunch for all I care." That's all I could think. It's *not* what I said. I said nothing.

"What about breakfast?" he asked.

"Breakfast? Well, how about if you buy your breakfast?"

"But, Mom, I'm hungry now."

I looked at the clock. It was almost time for the bus.

He looked at me like I had lost my mind. Usually I would cater to his every need, but I proceeded to shuffle stuff around in the fridge to see what I could throw together for him to take. A leftover slice of pizza, an apple, cheese. Cheese with pizza? No, too much cheese.

"I hate apples," he said as he saw me reach for one.

"Well, it's good for you. Try it; maybe you'll change your mind."

"No," he said. "I hate apples."

"Well, you used to love apples."

"I hate them now."

I looked at him. He was wearing summer-weight khakis. "Daniel, you should wear jeans. It is wet and chilly out."

"I hate jeans."

I reached for his head and attempted to smooth down the "alfalfa tufts" that pointed east and west and then grabbed the glasses from his face and cleaned them. He wrenched away from me and headed for the door.

"Did you brush your teeth?" I called after him. He ignored me.

I walked over to him. "Did you brush your teeth?"

"No," he said. "No time."

He grabbed his coat, and his book bag and left. The door slammed in my face. The perfect punctuation to the perfect fourteen-year-old departure. Why should this morning be unlike any other morning?

I called down the hall, "It's Picture Day. You should brush your teeth."

He ignored me and kept walking. I watched his trailing book bag round the corner and disappear.

"I love you!" I called out.

I sat down on the couch staring at Gracie as if she would explain to me how I could get her to make before I left for the gym. Then I heard water dripping. I looked at the large window in the living room and there it was—the water. As it dripped, it pooled and as it pooled, it poured over the side of the sill and onto the couch and the Persian rug. I called the doorman who didn't answer. I grabbed Gracie (since I didn't want to leave her for two minutes thinking she would have another "accident") and stormed down to the lobby.

I had called for a 10:00 a.m. meeting at work, which wasn't going to happen. I dialed my assistant and asked her what else was on the schedule.

"Sam," she said.

"Sam. Oh, Sam. OH, GOD," I thought. I can't cancel Sam. "Okay, make a reservation for 1:15 please, and call him to confirm. Thanks. What else?"

"12 noon. Chris."

"Chris. Chris who?"

"I don't know."

"Who's in the meeting?"

"You told me to schedule a meeting with everyone. You just said 'Chris' meeting."

"Okay. Whatever. I'll be there soon."

"And don't forget you have that issue with Marcia to sort out."

Oh yeah, the lawsuit that was being levied against us for the mistake a colleague made.

"Oh, and Mark is coming in tonight."

Oh yes, Mark—the TV series we were creating, maybe. Mark. That meant hair, nails, and dinner plans.

The rain was pouring down in sheets. Gracie was looking at me as if I were Cruella DeVille, and she didn't know what was next, but she knew it wasn't going to be good.

"Okay, girl, no gym for me today. Happy NOW?" I asked her.

I looked at the window and decided a couple of big bath towels and four Valiums would be way better than a bucket. But I don't take Valium and a bucket would be useless. I got showered, and dressed. The water would get dealt with somehow. I looked at the dog and pointed at her.

"Don't even THINK about leaving me any presents. I saved your life." And I left.

Now I was late and in need of a cab and there were of course no cabs in sight. I took the bus. I just stared out the window at the mess outside.

When I arrived at my office, my shoes were soaked, and yesterday's perfect blowout hung in strands around my face like the matted hair of a neglected doll. I threw my stuff down on the chair, and my cell phone rang. Daniel's school.

"Hello, Ms. Stretcher?" *Would they ever EVER get my name right?* "Daniel is fine, but, well, we have a little situation. On the form for Picture Day, you checked off that you wanted Daniel to have his picture taken with and without his cap and gown, but you can't have both. Which would you prefer?"

She didn't really think I cared? Did she? God, give me a break. Of course she did; she thinks I am an attentive responsible mother—of course I care.

"Hmmmm." I stalled, and watched the blinking lights of the incoming calls as if I were being tested and I actually could not think of the correct answer. "What does Daniel want?"

"Well, he wanted us to call you. He wants what you want."

"Tell him it's his choice; it's *his* picture, and he can have it any way he wants it," I answered. "What did I pay for?"

"Well, we don't know because the amount you sent was wrong for both selections."

"Okay, well, can you just pick something and let me know if I owe anything," I said and hung up.

My assistant's voice came over the intercom. "NBC, top line; Nickelodeon, on the bottom."

My cell phone rang again. I stared at it. Housekeeper. Better answer. "Hold them."

"Hello, Robyn?" It was my housekeeper's voice.

"Yes, Merle."

"Do you still want me to take Daniel for his haircut today?"

"Haircut? Oh? Uh, I thought that was *yesterday*." I then realized, today was Picture Day and I had made the haircut appointment for the wrong day.

"No, Merle, let it go. It's pouring out. Gotta run."

"About Gracie," she said.

"What about Gracie?"

"Well, she had an accident."

OF COURSE she had an accident. "I'm sorry you have to deal with that, but can you tell me about it later?"

I looked at the two lines blinking. Geneva's voice came over the intercom again.

"Who do you want first?"

No one. I didn't want anyone. I wanted a white prince to ride into my life and take me to a warm island, far away from all this, away from the phones and the rain and the dark mornings and the cold tiles. I wished more than anything in the world that I could crawl back into a bed and that when I woke up, I would be wrapped in someone's arms—someone who knew how to make the coffee, even if love was out of the question. I wished that Gracie would be fully trained, and that today wasn't Picture Day.

My cell phone rang again. Daniel on his cell phone from school.

"Hi, Sweetie."

"Hi, Mom."

"Is school over? No, it's too early. How was the picture?"

"No, no picture. I just wanted you to know—"

"Why, did I do something wrong on the form?" All I could think was that I had messed something else up.

"Well, it was cancelled because of the rain, so Picture Day will be tomorrow."

I sighed. "Oh, that's really too bad." I bit my tongue.

"Yeah, I know." He giggled. "I love you, Mom."

"Love you, too, Daniel. I am sure you will take a great picture tomorrow."

CHAPTER TWELVE

Boarding School

It was an August Sunday. The sky was an azure blue. The sun was the color of the brightest yellow crayon and made me squint. The ride went fast because I was doing eighty-five. I was listening to *I Drove All Night*. I loved Celine Dion's determination, and the song's relentlessness. I was singing along. I had just celebrated my forty-eighth birthday. I pulled over at a rest stop because I drank too much coffee. I looked in the mirror to fix my lipstick and I noticed how tired I looked. I was speeding the whole way and made good time, but I was worried. The nurse at Daniel's new boarding school said his eye was swollen and he was covered with a rash. I told her to take him to a doctor. I told her the cost was irrelevant and to do so right away. That was yesterday, but she didn't do it. She didn't listen. Now he was in the emergency room.

I had been in these situations before—alone, handling things, making decisions, and bridging the gap when the distance between Daniel and me was so great and I felt I couldn't get there fast enough, when I had to trust others with my son's care. I have survived these times: 9/11, summers of sleep-away camp, flights to visit relatives, and three schools, all of which required at least an hour on the bus in each direction. This was different. This wasn't a skinned knee I could clean, or a bully's mean comments I could shoo away. This wasn't a headache, a cough, or a cold. Something was very wrong. Why hadn't this nurse taken him to a doctor right away? It takes seconds to reverse years of planning. I knew this too well. It takes seconds for a whole life to change. We think life is structured on steel beams, but no, all of life hangs by threads and rubber bands and sometimes the threads break. Sometimes we bounce back, and sometimes we don't.

Maybe I am fearful that harm will come to those I love because my sister unexpectedly died when she was thirty-four. She had been given six to nine months to live and that is exactly how long it took before she could no longer fight the cancer. When that happened, my life had become a casino. I felt I was gambling or bargaining most of the time. If Daniel is okay, do I let him stay? Do I bring him home? *Okay,* I told myself, *I will have to calm down and see how the school administrators will handle this now that I will soon be up there.*

The emergency room doctor said on the phone he would be fine. I spoke with Daniel in the hospital. His voice was cheerful.

He said, "Don't worry, Mom. I'll be back at school soon."

I was driving fast. I needed to be with him. My thoughts were racing. If someone would have shown me a picture and told me this would have been my life, I would have laughed. I would have thought that person was crazy. I came to New York enthusiastic and thriving on the excitement of the city, and nothing would stop me. In my early thirties, I was newly married to a man with whom it seemed I would travel the world. We had a wonderful home and had everything to be hopeful for. My career in the entertainment industry was taking off. I had managed to fulfill my dream of living and making it here in New York. I had been diagnosed with a benign but large tumor in my head and had come through it. That was the first wake-up call. I didn't know it then but all that ambition and resourcefulness was the bedrock for the identity I would fall back on. It gathered its edges and form from places far and foreign to my former self long before I was a mother. Motherhood. Another wake-up call.

I remembered pushing Daniel in his stroller in Park Slope, willing to accept that we had challenges, but I wanted to really live, whether we were walking, riding bikes, sleeping, singing, laughing, or taking music and dance classes. Even through the hours of research and doctors, and all the unanswered questions, I was holding on to whatever we had when we were with each other. I found out I was very strong. I found out I could also retreat into the shadows. I was looking for the light now because at that very moment, I wanted to kill someone at that school.

The boarding school Daniel was attending specialized in educating students with various neurological and social issues. His educational and IQ testing had not changed since he was three; he had great strengths and great vulnerabilities. I likened it to a Swiss cheese—when you're on solid ground, you know just where you are, and when you're in a hole, you're gone. A high verbal IQ is half the battle, whatever that means, but despite twelve years of therapies, I had accepted that Daniel would contend with lifelong challenges of speech, fine motor coordination, awkwardness, social differences, and processing issues. If it worked out, he would attend the school for four years, and then possibly transition into a local community college. He was so outgoing and self-confident, he could negotiate better than I could, and I was a talent agent!

Sending my son to boarding school wasn't an easy decision. Daniel was fourteen and had been attending The Lowell School, a small non-public special education school in Queens, New York, for the past four years. He had enjoyed an exceptional experience there and I was very torn about high school. As middle school was ending, I thought of my son in high school, needing a social life and a community he did not yet seem to have. So many of his school friends lived far from us and he did not even have one close friend who could come over and hang out. Since it was just me and Daniel, and we had no family nearby, and his only cousin lived in California, I thought that if he were in a boarding environment with other children whose needs were like his, he would forge friendships and have a community that could last for years. I liked the idea that the boarding school also offered a post-secondary program that would incorporate life skills and a community college to make a smoother transition for life after high school. BUT I also knew I would miss him terribly. This school in upstate New York was geographically desirable, close enough for me to visit and for Daniel to commute home on the weekends if he chose.

Nine months earlier we had driven up to the school. I knew it wasn't perfect. No place is. I spoke with my parents, with Regina Skyer, and with Dede Proujansky, the executive director of The Lowell School, who more than anyone knew how torn I was and how I had always looked out for Daniel's best interests. We discussed Daniel's social life and how he had a hard time maintaining friendships and how he had no one to hang out with at home. I thought about the fact that he would be coming home alone each day and sitting in the house doing homework and watching TV. It didn't feel like enough. I thought about all the classes I had enrolled him in over the years—the music and dance and drama and cooking and all the ways I could try to improve his life—but he had outgrown so many of the programs that were available. I churned the idea inside out and upside down and I did the math so many times, because I had no idea how I could afford the high cost of the tuition without any assistance. Daniel flip-flopped for a year, "Good idea, bad idea, good idea, bad idea…. I'm going to love it; I'm going to hate it…." And while I was ambivalent, I made the commitment for him to start that summer when he was fourteen.

I had seen a few schools, and I knew that leaving The Lowell School was going to be tough for both of us, but this boarding school was closest and it would be easy for Daniel to travel home by train. Daniel had been to sleep-away camp, and he was fairly independent when traveling alone. Alan was struggling with his illness and it seemed he was going to endure a very serious surgery soon, so this seemed to be another good reason. Maybe I could insulate Daniel from what I knew were going to be some tough years ahead.

I am my son's best friend, our little dog is the only sibling he has, and we have no family nearby. I often wondered how Daniel's life would unfold, striking the balance between his obvious strengths and the needs he would have for community. I made sure he went to private, small, special education schools and a special sleep-away camp so he would have community. I encouraged Daniel while he was still young to travel by himself to visit relatives.

Daniel still talks about how he always got free cookies around the neighborhood in Park Slope when he was little. He said it was because he was cute, and that is partly true—but Daniel figured out that by telling everyone it was his birthday every day, they gave him free stuff. Once when he was returning from Florida, his flight was delayed. As he stepped through the Jetway, I heard his distinctive voice loudly announcing that they were late and that he hoped the pilot realized that his mother was waiting and worried. As the flight attendant approached me, she shared that Daniel had offered to help the pilot out and fly the plane when he realized they would be late. Helping my son achieve his potential for independence was my mission.

When I got up to the school, I found Daniel in his dorm room. His face was very swollen and all red. His eye was swollen shut. I walked over to him and gave him a hug. I held onto him until he squirmed away. He had packed his things mostly by himself. I was surprised he was alone. He was in good spirits, and asking questions. The questions. Can he please stay till the last day? He had so many projects he wanted to finish. He had so many friends; he just couldn't leave. I explained that he should come home so I can take care of him. I explained that I was worried about him, and that we were leaving for vacation and he needed to be well.

I asked him to go to the office to get his cell phone. He left the room. I looked around. I couldn't understand how one of the most exclusive schools on the East Coast for children with special needs wouldn't have responded more quickly to an obvious allergic reaction. His throat could have closed up. I was quietly packing. Maybe I was overreacting. But I was the one. I had to decide. I knew how I felt. At the hospital they treated him with steroids. I asked the school administrator on the phone to make sure someone stayed with him, but he was left in his room alone over night. I was so angry. I didn't want to talk to anyone. No one came into his room to see me anyway. I ran a business. I was responsible to clients. Where was the accountability of this school? I sat on the floor and finished packing up Daniel's things. I sat down and put my face in my hands. I just wanted to cry. I went through so much to get him here. Daniel returned with the cell phone. I instructed him to help me with the bags. He was dutiful, and complied.

"Mom, everything is okay. I am fine."

Two students saw me struggling with the heavier bags. They came to assist. I thanked them. Daniel wanted to go out for lunch. Of course. He loved to go out to eat. He loved to invite people to go out with us or come over to our home for dinners. He loved pizza. I said, "Yes, we can go out. No, we cannot invite anyone. Yes, we have to leave. No, I cannot change my mind." He was smart. He would figure it out.

In the car on the way home we talked about how much he liked it there and he asked if he would be coming back in the fall. I put my hand on his thigh. He was still chattering away. I drove. I was tired, so tired. I stayed quiet. Behind my sunglasses, he couldn't see the tears in my eyes.

CHAPTER THIRTEEN

Gracie

One day as I was walking Gracie, she pulled me forward to sniff something. I noticed a dead pigeon on the ground, its neck broken and bent into a ninety-degree angle, its wings splayed, its little, three-toed feet sticking up in the air. There was a second pigeon circling the dead one. It was circling and circling frantically thrusting its head to and fro the way pigeons do, but the circling didn't stop, not even when I got close enough to say, "I am so sorry." The pigeon looked at me in desperation, as if it were asking for help. When I walked away my heart was aching for this bird whose life mate lay dead on the ground. Pigeons love unconditionally. I thought of how, like me, this pigeon might be alone forever. And then I looked at this sweet dog we had rescued and I thought this homeless waif probably never expected she'd ever become a princess. Miracles do happen.

It seemed very important to the real estate agent who rented me my post-marital home to tell me that there were many eligible men in our new building. As the single parent of an eight-year-old child with special needs, my odds of reconnecting were probably worse than the regular odds, but that was okay.

I told myself I had been beating the odds most of my life; it just might take a while.

That first year on my own, I had so much to do with furnishing our apartment, reestablishing my career, and making sure Daniel was stable, that there was almost no time to think about the prospects for dating. It seemed very important, however, to anyone who knew me, to tell me of every divorced and separated man they knew. My separation had felt like wandering in the desert for forty years and I felt like I had dragged my son with me in search of the land of Canaan. I wasn't so sure how soon I would be ready for someone else's version of Mr. Right.

There were a few bad dates and one guy I went out with for a few months who was very sweet, but it was obvious to me that none of them were ever going to meet my son; they were not destined to be a part of his life or a long-term part of mine. It had been almost two years since Alan and I had been separated, and I guess when I met Peter, I was ready.

I met Peter in Grand Central Station at a bar called The Campbell Apartment. When he kissed me after the second round of drinks, he figured I'd either slap his face, or reciprocate. I did the latter. Afterwards, he told me that I would have been right to slap his face, but it was too good a kiss to do that. If anything, I hoped that he'd do it again. He waited till after dinner, but the second time was even better than the first.

After a couple of months, I was juggling my time with Peter and Daniel, but somehow I wanted to merge these parts of my life. I wanted my son to know I was happily involved with a man, but I was nervous about introducing them. I feared that my son wouldn't accept a new man in my life or if he did that he would become overly attached, and then what? And I feared that Peter might not accept Daniel. It seemed so hard to describe my son. I casually invited Peter for pizza, Daniel's favorite. I told Daniel that a friend was coming over. When Peter arrived, Daniel was on the computer. I simply told him I wanted to introduce him to someone. Peter stood by the door and waved at him. Daniel waved back and that was that. I made drinks for us. We sat on the couch and had cocktails, and then we ate. Afterwards, Daniel went back to his computer. Peter and I looked at each other and he smiled at me and I figured it went fine. There wasn't a lot of discussion about Daniel's complexities. A relief. I didn't have to talk about it.

When Daniel got his hearing aids and didn't want to wear them, when he was diagnosed with Growth Hormone Deficiency and we had to administer nightly shots of growth hormone, when I would drop Daniel off at his dad's, slink down into my seat, and stare out the window, Peter was there. When we dropped Daniel at Summit Camp, Peter held me as I cried on our way home. Peter was at numerous school shows and awards dinners, and he and Daniel became good friends. Life wasn't uncomplicated, but complete with the rambunctious Boston terrier we got. And while none of us were perfect—not me, not Daniel, not Peter, and not the rambunctious dog—we did the best we could.

Eventually, I realized that although Peter and I loved each other, we were not destined for a lifetime partnership. At forty-six this was, once again, a terrifying step into the unknown. Once again, I was ending a relationship that would cause pain for all of us, but I couldn't make peace with the inner searching. I had to discover things about myself, even if I knew it would be hard. It was very hard. At first Daniel and I were both sad and he often asked me to get back with Peter, but eventually Daniel and I naturally slid into a lifestyle—pizza in front of the TV, finding our way, just the two of us. I kept assuring him, some families are just a mom and a kid and a dog and that it's okay. He didn't really believe that he and I were still a family. I couldn't handle Lucky, the Boston terrier, so that summer while Daniel was at camp, Lucky took up permanent residence with Peter.

I knew Daniel would be heartbroken and I had to find another dog, fast. Gracie became our rehabilitation project. She was the one who healed us from the loss of Peter and Lucky. She was Daniel's first being for whom he became responsible. As silly as it sounds, Gracie became my son's canine sister, and the little girl I never had. She would dutifully sleep with him each night and became the mute listener of all Daniel's problems and thoughts. She was by my side or at my feet wherever I was in the house, and I can't imagine life without her now, although it wasn't easy at first. She did not trust us and when we adopted her she had been seriously neglected and lived with a foster mother who had twenty other dogs. To say she had special needs is putting it lightly. She growled and bit her way through every grooming and training session, but now, she is a docile, loving princess. I remember telling Daniel early on that she wasn't a pitiful, homeless girl; she was royalty gone a bit astray seeking her kingdom.

When we got her home, I remember Daniel saying, "Welcome to your new home, Gracie. I am your brother and I will make sure nothing bad ever happens to you again."

CHAPTER FOURTEEN

Little Buddha

It was the day before Thanksgiving 2006, a hazardous day for travel. Daniel and I wove through Penn Station. I reminded myself to move at half my normal pace of five miles an hour. My son does not move quickly due in part to sensory integration issues that can heighten and sometimes impede the way he sees, hears, smells, and interprets space. This means a crowd might visually overwhelm him, a curb feels like it is ten feet off the ground, the wind might feel like a turbine engine, the brightness of the sun will blind him, a little bump will send him flying, an uneven sidewalk could cost him a skinned knee, and a small hill is his Everest.

According to Daniel, the reason he couldn't walk the dog is because if she stopped to poop he would step in it because he wouldn't see it and his lack of hand-eye coordination would make it hard for him to pick it up, but I was tired of listening to that excuse, and made sure he learned how to get it done. I am told Daniel has a severe astigmatism and so it is possible he wouldn't see the poop. I am not even sure how clearly he sees with his glasses on, and his hearing aids probably amplify sounds in a way that I wouldn't want to experience in a crowded place. When he takes them off it is like living with an old person. He can't hear me and I have to raise my voice to tell him that he needs to put his hearing aids on and turn the TV volume lower. Still, we *both* wander around losing our stuff. And even after eighteen years, I hear myself say as we walk, "C'mon, Daniel, stay with me. Don't trail behind. C'mon sweetie, we have to move...." You would think after all this time I would get that this is just the way it is. Perhaps it is hopefulness, and perhaps all that hopefulness is just a habit. Kind of like a marriage.

We were taking the train from Penn Station to Providence, Rhode Island, to spend Thanksgiving with my parents on Cape Cod. We descended the escalators into the station and were immediately absorbed into a sea of people. In scenes like this, I was always thinking about my son disappearing and tried to keep him in front of me. Then I imagined that if he were abducted, within minutes the person who did it would come looking for me in panic over how to answer the questions that come like water through a burst pipe—questions about why the traffic moves a certain way, why the trains run as they do, why there are so many people in Penn Station, and why we have to travel on such a crowded day (that is actually a great question).

I have tried to teach Daniel, "No stopping at the head of the subway stairs. Keep to the right when descending into the station. No standing in front of the train doors ever. Don't talk to me when the train is coming because I can't hear you."

There was the arguing—tolerable to me only because that is the only "normal" milestone my fifteen-year old had hit. Instead of being upset, I had to celebrate it. Though I had been secretly so grateful when all those "typically developed" kids were throwing tantrums and mine wasn't, it now was payback time. How could Daniel be so sure he was right and be so, so *wrong?* The only way to make him stop was to agree with his theory that a sugar-and-white-flour-and-cheese diet was good for him, and that brushing his teeth wasn't. I didn't defend my knowledge that watching too much TV is lazy and that he needed to exercise more. Indeed, a girl would one day like him and all that would change.

The worries about someone snatching him away from me were not my real worries. My real concerns were that all the luggage stayed in tow, and that as the crowds were growing and moving like stampeding cattle, my son wouldn't suddenly stop or trip, or that his rolling luggage did not suddenly twist away from him, or that someone behind him didn't fall down and break his or her neck because Daniel had come to a dead halt while everyone else was still moving.

We made our way through the masses to the ticket kiosk. I surveyed the area for the customer service center and Daniel followed.

As we approached the customer service center, Daniel asked, "Why are we here? We have our tickets."

I moved toward the desk and said to the woman in a somewhat matter-of-fact tone: "My son has special needs and we would like to be pre-boarded."

It is my well-practiced request to stay clear of very crowded places and get VIP service at places like Disney World, airports, cruise ships, and amusement parks. I am imagining thousands of people descending the stairs and escalators, pushing to get onto the platform and a very crowded train. I am sure that we have too much luggage as usual, and that I need a porter. I am imagining that we want to sit together—although that is probably something I desire more than my son. He would spend the entire five hours in the snack car.

From behind me I felt a strong yank on my coat. There was that defiant, fifteen-year-old demanding voice:

"MOM, WHY MUST YOU ALWAYS TELL PEOPLE I HAVE SPECIAL NEEDS? IF I GET TRAMPLED, I GET TRAMPLED. IT WILL BE MY PROBLEM, NOT YOURS!"

I turned and smiled and thought, "No dear, no. It won't be solely your problem if you get trampled, it will be *my* problem. I am the one who will have to fend off the tramplers and then pick up your broken body and that is not how I am starting *my* long weekend."

"Well, why can't we just see what happens? Why can't we give it a try?"

For half a second I actually considered it, and then I decided, no, I am too selfish. I didn't trust the herding crowds in Penn Station on the day before Thanksgiving for my son's experiment as to whether he would or wouldn't be trampled. But in my heart I understood how badly he just wanted to be like everyone else.

"No. We have too much stuff we are lugging and I am not taking chances. The train will be crowded and I want to sit together."

"Whatever," he said and looked away disgusted. It made me feel badly.

As we moved through the crowd to the waiting area where we would be escorted onto the train, I didn't mind sitting with elderly people and a blind man and his companion. Hanging out in the section where people have special needs, I always notice someone who has it so much "worse," whatever that means. I look around at other typical families, I think: My picture books are far from perfect, more like collages than snapshots. So be it. Mine was far from the typical suburban "soccer mom" images of driving carpools to and from a house in a town somewhere with two cars in a garage, a few kids in tow, and a husband waiting. If that was ever the life I ever dreamed of, I long ago abandoned the idea that it was meant for me. Whatever the cost, however lonely it ever gets, the places I will travel to are rich with moments unlike any other. I will go to the edge of who I am, and if I have any hopes or dreams, it is that my son will discover within himself that same yearning. And I know that no matter where I go or he goes, he will be in my heart if not by my side.

A cab driver recently told me that Daniel was a "seer."

"A seer," I asked, "what is a seer?" I was thinking he meant a prophet, which I found interesting since Daniel in some religions was a prophet.

He said my son could see through foreheads and palms.

He said, "Your son, he is very special. He is *very, very* special. Special like Gandhi or Buddha!"

He said one day I would remember this cab ride when my son was very famous. Maybe it will come true, who knows, or maybe he just wanted a bigger tip. Maybe one day my son will use this as an excuse as to why he couldn't get his math homework done—because he is already like Gandhi or Buddha.

CHAPTER FIFTEEN

Hold on Tight

My son lay unconscious next to me. It was the first time I rode in an ambulance. Earlier that morning, he had said he was very tired and couldn't go to school. I wasn't too concerned and just told him to go back to bed. I proceeded to get ready for work. When I emerged from the bathroom where I had been drying my hair, I called to Daniel but he didn't answer. I went into his room where I found him lying on the floor face down. At first I thought he was fooling around. I said his name, but he didn't respond. I said it louder, nothing. I leaned over and shook him, and then I shook him frantically, nothing.

"Oh my God," I heard myself say. "Oh my God." I grabbed the phone and dialed 911. I ran to my neighbor. He came in and checked Daniel's pulse and breathing. I kneeled next to my son; his unresponsiveness was terrifying. My one hand on his forehead, I held his hand in my other hand as we waited for the EMS people. The dog was sitting by us very dutifully, but unable to tell me what had happened.

When they came, one of them conjectured that Daniel had had a seizure. Since my son had no history of seizures and he was fifteen, it seemed odd to me, but I agreed it seemed like that was what had happened. There was no evidence of a fall or damage to his head or mouth; that was the good news. It appeared he had rolled out of bed and was probably unconscious before he hit the floor. There he lay, IVs in his arm, in what seemed like a deep sleep.

The ambulance ride was long, and I will never look at an ambulance racing through the streets the same way again. I held on to Daniel's hand. "Hold on tight, honey, hold on." I remembered the ride over the Brooklyn Bridge before I had ever met my son, fearing I would lose him and yet knowing somehow, we would one day be very close.

"Hold on, baby, hold on," I whispered.

As the emergency workers wheeled Daniel into the hospital, he started to come to, but was very disoriented as if he were coming out of a very deep sleep.

The day before was like any other day. I had walked through Lord & Taylor, searching for pants for him. Daniel was now fifteen, finishing his first year back at The Lowell School where he was now in high school. After the boarding school incident, I was relieved that Lowell was willing to offer a much coveted spot for him in school. We were very fortunate. He was so happy to be back with his familiar teachers and at school with the kids he knew. I had been thinking about the jacket, tie, and shirt I would buy him to wear for his year-end awards ceremony. I had been thinking of his first year in high school. High school, how did that happen? I remembered the words of Daniel's principal when he first interviewed at The Lowell Middle School five years earlier. Daniel was entering fifth grade and I had begged the admissions director to see him, knowing the school interviews only eight or ten incoming students of a given age. I remembered my nervousness each time we had to change schools and my fear. I remembered feeling like a marketing director. After Daniel had passed muster with the director of admissions at Lowell, she had called the principal for a once-over and within minutes, the principal looked at me and smiled. "I see no reason why Daniel won't fit in perfectly here at Lowell." I had never heard those words before. I had no idea how he would get from class to class dragging that heavy book bag. I had no idea how he wouldn't lose everything he had—computer, hearing aids, glasses, homework, books, and himself in the process—but with the help, guidance, sense of humor, and patience of the Lowell staff, my lost, late, and unprepared son began to congeal into the resemblance of a fairly functional high school student.

I thought back over his four years of middle school. I thought of how Daniel had won so many awards. He sang in chorus, won an award for journalism, made honor roll, fell in love, even figured out how to run up a tab at the pizza place.

The day I found out about the pizza incident, a very nervous Daniel was pacing. He blurted out, "Did the principal call you?"

"Why would the principal call?"

"Well, I can't tell you."

"Okay, then don't tell me."

"Well, I told her I would tell you."

"OKAY then, do tell me."

"Well, I can't."

"Well, this could go on all night Daniel."

And then the tears came. He confessed that he was sure he would drive Vinnie, the owner, out of business, he sobbed hysterically. He had been spending his pizza money for breakfast, and for months, Vinnie had taken pity on Daniel thinking he couldn't afford his pizza, and had been giving him free slices. Daniel could barely finish the story. It was the first time my son had done something so deviant, but his dramatic remorse was so comical, I wasn't sure how to respond.

"Well, Daniel. I really want to help you, so when you stop crying we can try to find a solution."

He just went into his room, and threw himself down on the bed where I could hear his crying. I went in to console him. His face was red and he looked very tired.

"So, how are we going to solve this problem?" I asked him.

"I can't solve the problem."

"Of course you can. Let's figure out how much you owe Vinnie and then you can go over there, pay him back and earn the money back so you can pay me back the money you will give him."

A simple math exercise revealed that Daniel owed roughly $35. We had agreed he would do some chores around the house for the money and pay Vinnie back.

I thought back to the end of middle school. There was an award given to a single student for outstanding courage, commitment, and community involvement. I had sat there listening to the child they were describing and thought of how those parents would be so happy. I was so moved to hear of the strengths, concern for others, generosity, kindness, determination, and sense of humor this child possessed. Most parents concern themselves with what their children's future will look like, but for those of us who parent complex children, our concerns are not what they will do *when* they make it—we didn't know *if* our kids will make it. As the winner of the Triple C award was announced, I thought of how proud those parents would be. I looked into the sea of young faces for the child who had demonstrated these admirable traits. And then I heard my son's name echoing across the room. Daniel jumped out of his seat and ran to the podium. There were tears in his eyes. I just sat there and sobbed.

That was only last year, I thought, but it seemed so long ago.

I was jolted back to the present by my son's voice. He had been passed out for about an hour.

"Hey, what am I doing here?"

"You were unconscious; do you remember anything? We are in an emergency room."

He looked at the IV. A nurse was monitoring his every breath and heartbeat. The nurses and doctors had no idea what to make of it, nor did I, but I was grateful that Daniel recognized me. He started to pull on the tubes.

"Stop, Daniel. Calm down."

"No. Wait a minute, my awards ceremony is tonight. Hey, I am NOT staying in this hospital!"

It was a good sign. Of course, we would go to the awards ceremony. It never occurred to me that if it were a seizure he could have another one. I was just so happy he was okay. About an hour later, the attending physician who released us told me to follow up with our neurologist. As the nurses were unhooking Daniel from his tubes and IV, I realized he didn't have shoes on. Daniel was so preoccupied with the awards ceremony that neither his ambulance ride nor his missing shoes were of interest to him.

"Daniel, you don't have shoes. Wait a minute." He was already off the bed and reaching for his pajama top.

"C'mon Mom, they'll give me some slippers. Who cares? I'll go out barefoot. Let's just get out of here." And he began walking toward the door.

Of course, we were going to the awards ceremony that night. We wouldn't miss it for anything.

CHAPTER SIXTEEN

For Every Pot There Is a Cover

Daniel emerged from the prom, his shirt a bit disheveled, forehead a bit sweaty, tie a bit crooked, but his jacket was still on.

"How was it?" I asked.

"Okay," he said.

"Doesn't sound very convincing. Everything *really* okay?"

"Well, I asked this girl to dance with me and I ruined her night."

"How did you ruin her night by dancing with her?"

"Well, we were on the dance floor, and I twirled her and I twirled her and I was twirling her so hard she tripped."

"Well, did you twirl her maliciously?" I asked this knowing that the girl had another boyfriend and that Daniel wished it could be him.

"No, I would never do that. I was just so joyful."

"Okay, so then what?"

"I left."

"You left her on the dance floor?"

"Well, I was so upset with myself I just walked away."

"What did she do?"

"She followed me out and asked me if I was okay. "

"Well, if you had ruined her night she wouldn't have asked you if you were okay."

He sat in the back, staring out the window in silence.

"I am sorry, honey."

"I am so stupid."

"No, you aren't; being joyful is never stupid."

I sat in the front seat wishing I could tell my son how proud of him I was—that despite his fruitless efforts at securing a date, he chose to go to the prom alone. I wanted him to know how brave he was, that most kids lack the self-confidence he has, and that the girl with whom he had been dancing was only one of many girls who might be "the one." But I knew this wouldn't salve his wounded seventeen-year-old heart.

It is not easy being a parent, being a single parent, being a woman raising a teenage boy, and raising a teenage boy with special needs. I am his mother and nothing I could say would be right. Long ago he reminded me: Love is complicated.

I read the wedding announcements with the same commitment some people read the obituaries. I am searching for inspiration. I see past the poses and the smiles; I see the challenges of cultural diversity, same sex unions, and older women marrying younger men. In these strangers' nuptial snippets lie their challenges, frailties, and faults. I see what they overcame to get there. The ten-year anniversary of my divorce is coming up. I feel excommunicated at times from anything marital, in some ways from anything mainstream. In the same way Daniel seeks the love of his life, I thought I would have been remarried by now.

After years of searching the nuptial pages, one photo is missing—the photo of the couple with something that obviously, outwardly identifies them as being challenged, different, or complex. If ever I find it, I will cut it out and put it in my drawer to remind me that my son will find his intended, the one who will love him long after I am gone. I am looking for a guarantee, for both of us, because for different reasons, I think I, too, must be complex. I want the promise fulfilled that "For every pot there is a cover."

When I took my wedding vows, I was sure I would keep them. But things happen—life changes us and sometimes makes it impossible for us to keep our promises. If ever I dreamed about the safety of a well-provisioned life in a suburb with carpools, a few kids, two cars in the garage, a second home, and by now twenty-five anniversaries' worth of jewelry and cards in a drawer somewhere from a sole predictable source, that dream is gone. Unlike my parents, I will never celebrate a fiftieth anniversary—maybe not even a twenty-fifth. If ever that was the life I dreamed of, I have long ago abandoned the idea that there are sole sources of anything. Predictability was never meant for me. I have made my peace with that departure. I wasn't perfect. I became a statistic. When I look at my wedding photo, hidden in our blissful smiles is what we didn't know. I wasn't perfect, nor was he, and one too many turns to the left or right made it harder and harder to stay.

That first year on my own, I cried a lot. I think Daniel cried, too, but it wasn't easy to get him to talk about it. I wondered if he would forgive my seemingly selfish quest for fulfillment—a quest I could hardly articulate to myself, let alone to an eight-year-old challenged with his own issues and divorce. In my weakest moments I wondered if I made a bad mistake, but in my stronger moments I trusted that my inner navigational system hadn't malfunctioned. I had better things in mind for both of us. I won't lie. A year into being alone, I longed for romantic nights. I longed to be told how I was beautiful, sexy, wanted, and needed. Sometimes, I felt like I was fleeing, manic like a refugee. Other times, I was well-stocked, centered, searching for a love I had yet to find. I knew I wasn't short on commitment, or loyalty, or dedication; I had to keep my faith in love, but I had to keep up with my life, too. I had to keep Daniel on track. Every parent-teacher meeting, every academic triumph, every organizational coup, every wave of the mascara wand, every new lipstick, every pair of shoes, and every trip to the gym were all part of the heroic regimen for "super single mom"—balancing, child, work, and self. My only prayer was that my complex son would somehow come out okay from all this and learn his own brand of independence.

Then the day came when I started crying. I am not sure how long Daniel stood by the doorway watching.

His voice surprised me, "What's wrong?"

"I am sad." I wasn't sure he had ever seen me cry.

"Why?"

"I am tired of being alone."

"You have me."

"Yes honey, I have you. Thank God, I have you."

"If you feel alone, maybe you should have some dates."

I sniffled.

Maybe he was right. So, I went out on dates. Lots of dates. Sometimes I was so disappointed I was sure I would spend the rest of my life alone but I could *never ever* let my son know I felt this way.

One day when Daniel was fifteen, he and I were deep in conversation about a girl who was showing him no interest.

"I am a kind, generous, good-hearted person. I am so nice. Why is it that she does not see this in me? What could she possibly want?"

I wish I knew.

"I must be ugly," he said.

"No, you are not ugly, and when you are older, you will meet the right girl and she will see the beauty of your soul," I offered.

"I think you should get married again, Mom." He was changing the subject.

"Why do you think that?"

"Because it would make me happy."

I wasn't so sure. A lot of time had gone by.

Soon after that conversation, I hired an executive matchmaking firm—which failed to produce even a single appropriate prospect. And at forty-eight, I had not sat in a bar alone for twenty years, and wasn't deluding myself into thinking that was how I was going to meet the man of my dreams either.

One night, after a terrible ice storm caused our living room window to come crashing in, I went out for a drink. When the bartender came over, I looked into his eyes, and thought, *very handsome.*

I sat there drinking slowly, pretending to watch the baseball game. Really, I watched my bartender, whose name I learned was Jim. When I asked to borrow the reading glasses that hung from his shirt, I wondered if we had anything in common. I was fishing for clues about how I could justify making small talk with a bartender.

By my second drink and a salad, I had learned that bartending was his weekend gig and that during the week he worked in sales and had two children to whom he seemed committed. The more liquor I consumed, the commonalities mounted, or maybe I just hoped they were mounting. We shared a strong work ethic and devotion to our children. Neither of us wore rings on our left hands. I am, however, wise enough to know it meant nothing. There were plenty of single women who came and went from a place like this, and a handsome bartender would have to know how to keep the ladies coming back. I shocked myself that I had given it any thought.

Neighborhood people came and went. I never left my perch. After a rotation of light-weight conversations, including a stalker whom I had fantasized my bartender would punch in the face, and a long-winded one-sided conversation with a nice guy who knew a lot about movies, Jim offered to buy me a drink.

"If I drink one more, someone has to walk me home."

"Okay, how 'bout I buy you that drink and I walk you home?" he offered.

Outside, I felt myself swaying and appreciated that he steadied me. We stopped a few feet from my door. I wanted to show him the view from my roof, and without warning, I took him by the hand and let him into the building. He willingly followed. Once we were outside on the roof, he took me in his arms, and began kissing me. I don't know how long we were there. It was the quietest I had been all night. And then, afterwards, in the awkward silence, he asked me if he could take me out the following week. He said he would call over the weekend.

The next morning, all I could think was, "you stupid fool, you kissed a bartender and he works nearby—and you gave him your number. You have lost your mind."

Three days later, there were a dozen roses and a note from him on my dining room table. "I would have called Sunday, but at 2:00 a.m., without my reading glasses, I was definitely challenged. Your number never made it into my phone. I feel a little stupid, so please accept my apology." His number was on the bottom. I liked his choice of the word "challenged."

A good friend of mine said, "Doors open, doors close…" It never dawned on me until later that both of us could have bolted. A lost phone number was an automatic out. I read his note three times before I called. I thought about the reading glasses I had borrowed and the kiss. Common ground.

When I came down to the lobby for our first date, his smile was so warm and sweet, I thought I'd trip. When he took me by the hand I thought, "I could hold another man's hand, and it will never feel this way."

There is a certain comfort in the way we finish each other's sentences, or come to a full stop at exactly the same second to observe a pink sky or a moon over the East River. If you see us walking hand-in-hand, stopping to kiss each other, you might wonder how long we have been together, a lifetime or a minute. Sometimes it feels like both.

One day I overheard Daniel grilling Jim. "How long have you been with my mother?"

"Why?"

"Are you taking her out for your anniversary?"

"Yes, I am."

"Are you going to ask my mother to marry you?"

"Daniel, I am sure I will spend the rest of my life with your mother."

"I know, but are you going to ask her to marry you?"

"Well, someday, when the time is right I will."

"When will the time be right?'

I snuck away from the door, knowing the inquisition might not end so soon. Daniel saw a lifetime partner in this proposition, too, a lifetime partner who would share his love of baseball.

I read the wedding announcements each Sunday, hoping Daniel and I both make it to those pages. My photo will announce to the world my triumph over the complexities of my life and loves. But in the picture of my special son , a young man for whom love triumphs over all, I will see he has found the one with whom he was destined to live out his days, the woman he is to love and honor and cherish. I will know he has found the one who will love him long after I am gone. In Daniel's wedding photo, I will know it is true, "For every pot there is a cover."

CHAPTER SEVENTEEN

A View From the Mirror

I stood in front of the mirror on Daniel's eighteenth birthday. We were going to Yankee Stadium to watch my son's beloved team in the 2009 play-offs. As I brushed my teeth, he stepped behind me. How did he get so tall? How did he get so big? How did he become a man? I looked him over. He was wearing a black cashmere sweater, his shirt was tucked into his neatly pressed jeans, and his face was clean shaven. I could not believe his face needed to be shaved daily now. How did that happen? I smiled at him, turned around and said, "You look very handsome."

I tried to remember how I felt when, thirty-three years earlier, I had turned eighteen and moved to New York to attend college. I was excited and scared, and in many ways, even with all the social skills and drive I had, I know I was not as emotionally secure as my son seems to be. As I stood there putting on my makeup, I saw the mother I became, the business woman I am, and the woman I grew to be. But all those years ago, I never would have believed that my life would become what it did.

I am often asked how I knew what to do. I am asked how I came to know and intuit my son's needs, how I came to embrace him with all of his complexities.

I didn't know what to do or how to mother him, really. I just tried not to let the worries and concerns take over. I looked for things to celebrate and laugh about, like the day we were in the park when Daniel was three and had to "go." So, I did what any self-respecting mother would do—I taught him to find a tree. Indeed, as we faced that tree and I tried to explain—which, of course, was silly because *I* had no first-hand experience with this—I leaned into him from behind trying to keep his feet from getting wet. Just as he was getting the hang of it (no pun), my son, lacking concentration and fine motor skills, saw his nursery teacher walking by. He turned and started to wave and, of course, we both got wet. Teaching my son to pee on a tree in a public park was NOT what I wanted his teacher to see. There were no guide books to read, there was no one to help really, and I guess I just had to find the way for both of us. It never occurred to me that there was any choice. I didn't know it then, but now I think the bond I feel with my son had been forged in those first moments of his conception, in those life-altering seconds when I began this journey into a life I never expected.

When I look at my son, I don't see an awkward eighteen-year-old who can't handwrite well or ride a bike. I only know that whatever he dreams, I listen. I listen to his ideas, I read his screenplays, I marvel at his insights and commentary on baseball and politics. I listen when he says he wants to be a baseball player or an announcer some day. I gave birth to a dreamer. I guess it is my job to show him the process for his dreams to come true. No one would ever guess how many evaluations or doctor appointments we endured, how much scrutiny this young man has undergone in his young life. I had made up my mind very early on not to dwell on any of the outcomes. I made it the doctors' job to find out the information they wanted and I sifted through their conclusions carefully and skeptically. They could have their tests, but it was obvious to me that my information would come from my son.

When not one but two orthodontists wanted to break my son's jaw and pull some teeth down surgically, I realized that neither of them was from the school of "let's see what Daniel has to say about this." They had no intention of being willing to wait and see. But "wait and see" had become our way of life, so their suggestion was out of the question. And, indeed, the following year the missing teeth were in place without intervention and Daniel's bite was so good he gained twelve pounds. I guess that was the worst $1600 in consultation fees I ever spent—just for two bad opinions!

I never wanted to become Daniel's therapist. I was determined to let all his therapies take place at school or with professionals at their offices. My job was to love my son. Sometimes when I worked late away from my office, I would sneak into a restroom to talk to my son, or I would race home just in time before sleep overcame him so I could whisper how much I loved him and blow the worries from his head. Little did I know that every one of our bedtime talks was a type of therapy for both of us, because as we talked we learned who we were. No one knew how I prayed in the dark hours of solitude that somehow, whatever I was doing, our lives would work. In those years of so much unknown, I hid my insecurities well, and I told myself, there are no rights and wrongs—just a bunch of paths you take, hoping you do the right thing, and a couple of u-turns later, there's another possibility.

My life isn't filled with the same fears now as when Daniel was little. I have come through all the agonizing unknowns of a young child whose development lies in uncertainty, and I have made choices that have taught me my self-confidence. I don't have the answers about what lies ahead. Daniel *will* come through as he always has. I don't know how this child who couldn't hold a crayon navigates now so independently, but as long as there is a microwave, money so he can buy his mac-and-cheese and Skinny Cow treats, and someone to fold his clothes, make his bed, and get him up in the morning, and as long as there is baseball to watch or a conversation about it to have, then life is good. He does get his homework done most of the time and I don't help.

When he was in eighth grade I told Daniel every grade he earned was his, his to be proud of, or his to be unhappy about. I hated homework when I got it, and I would hate it no less if I sat there and did it perfectly for my capable child. I trusted that if he were given an assignment, he could follow through. If on occasion he were unable to deliver a finished assignment, I would send him back to school, homework incomplete, to his teacher. I counseled Daniel to communicate that he was not being lazy but that he lacked the appropriate information to get the homework done. During one brief period, I did help Daniel with his math that he was struggling with, and later the teacher told me Daniel was getting a math tutor. I was thrilled. When I met with the math tutor, he asked what Daniel's homework habits were. I told him I was so concerned, I was helping Daniel. He suggested I stop immediately, since in class Daniel was a hundred percent capable of doing the assignments, and he told me that clearly, something was happening at home that was impeding his performance. I learned my lesson. I feel very strongly about this metaphor for homework and life—If a child is being "hand-held" through homework, there will never be an accurate picture of where his or her academic functioning lies. I would rather know the truth about my son's abilities, rather than have him *appear* to be capable (or incapable) and not having earned his own grades. We recently learned Daniel passed all the tests for his New York State Regional Diploma eligibility—not bad for a kid whom the best educational consultant in New York predicted might not read and would be "very difficult to educate." We have The Lowell School to thank for shepherding Daniel through the past eight years of academic successes.

How did Daniel manage to keep his composure when, throughout sixth grade, he was bullied daily? He never even told me—a teacher did. The same child who sat alone year after year and kept to himself, now plans dinner parties and won a student council election against the most popular kid. Somehow he accumulated enough self-confidence and coping skills to negotiate all those free pizza slices from unsuspecting Vinnie—the pizza guy.

Daniel is the kid who would have fallen down if he ran three steps, but last winter, while we were in Sarasota watching a baseball practice, Daniel started running with a crowd in pursuit of one of the player's autographs. When he was little, I would not have been able to watch that without fearing for his life but there he was beating out some of the other runners. When they reached their destination, they all piled against a fence yelling for the player's attention. I could hear Daniel's once high-pitched voice bellowing.

"Hey," he called as he scaled a fence. When had his voice become so deep?

Is that MY son on that fence? I ran to him, and pushed my way through the mob, thinking he would fall. As he hung over the top of the fence he yelled,

"Hey, Mister! My mother is SO HOT. Come over here!" I could not believe what I was hearing, but then again, he was seventeen. And in that way, he was as typical as it gets!

In those hours before sleep comes to me, I wonder who I might have been, and who I'll never be. Am I still a valuable commodity in a business driven by youth and beauty? Am I "cool?" Am I enough—hot enough, rich enough? I conclude probably none of the above but I accept that. I just hope I am a good mother; I hope I am patient enough and smart enough to figure out what's next. I have observed parents of children my son's age immersed in the competition of the college process, agonizing over their kids' pursuits of getting into the best schools, and hoping for scholarships. My son may never go to a university, law school or medical school, and we won't be writing college essays about his accomplishments. But I would tell anyone who would listen that my son is a good man. A man who is there for his father as he battles cancer, a man with a sense of commitment that has me both impressed and filled with awe. Daniel's inimitable branded presence captivates everyone in school and in the neighborhood, from our doorman to the video store clerk, who both listen to his encyclopedic knowledge about baseball. How did he learn all that? I have no idea. Maybe one day he will make some money with all he knows—hopefully legally.

Daniel taught me humility, he taught me to love myself, he taught me not to give up, he taught me that the hardest things are worth delving into, he taught me to listen and to pay attention and to trust. He taught me unconditional love. Recently I received a call from a client. Her newborn son had had a seizure. When I heard her breaking voice I knew I had to go see her. It was nighttime when I wandered into the Neonatal Intensive Care Unit of a New York City hospital. It was so much quieter and more peaceful than when my own son was in the NICU. I peeked at the babies. They were all fairly quiet. I listened to the beeps and whooshes of their life-saving equipment. I didn't see any mothers or fathers. I smiled at a nurse, a nice nurse. She asked whom I was there to see. I didn't remember any nice nurses from my son's time in the NICU but I am sure they were *all* very nice and just doing their jobs. At that time I didn't exactly trust anyone.

I summoned every inch of strength I had because I never expected I'd be in another NICU and didn't want to cry. I smiled again at that nurse and remembered how I would have slept on a floor, with my IV attached to me, just to be near my son. Of course, in retrospect I know why they sent the hospital social worker to see me. I didn't make the best impression. I guess the hormones and the morphine were all conspiring along with my will, but I have later decided that we have to become unreasonable with ourselves and those around us from time to time to get what we want. And yes, I was a bit unreasonable.

It was eighteen years later, and I realized it was the first time I had been back in this place—this place where the unimaginable happens, where everything you expected becomes everything you could never have expected, where a baby sleeps in your arms and you wonder who will the baby look like, will he or she be happy, dance, sing, have talents and intelligence? I looked into the eyes of this beautiful young mother and I saw her grace and her fear and her love. I looked at her newborn son hooked up to electrodes and I saw Daniel, at fifteen after his seizure, one minute lying in my arms and the next, sitting upright in a hospital bed demanding to go to his awards ceremony. I wished I could show her a picture of who her boy would become, how brave he would be. I wished I could promise her that her boy would move through the world touching all who knew him the way Daniel had, because I knew it was possible. I had lived it. I held her tight and I was holding myself, all those years ago.

CHAPTER EIGHTEEN

A Letter from Daniel

October 6, 2009.

*M*y *life is different than other kids I know because I have to type my homework every single night instead of writing by hand. Sometimes I notice I walk a weird way. I wouldn't necessarily call it weird but to other people it might seem weird. I still do like gym, but I didn't do that well in basketball. But I am good at kickball. I get on base a lot. But I really do like baseball the best. The thing about baseball for me is that I have a want to be a baseball player. It is a dream a lot of people think is impossible, but I think it is possible. I take baseball lessons once a week and my knowledge about baseball is very good because I have taught myself a lot about it.*

Making friends was a challenge for me in middle school, but I refused to give up hope, and I worked on my people skills. I tried to pay attention to what people's different needs were. Now that I am in high school, I have some great friends.

My greatest gift is that I am always happy and that I make the best of almost every situation. I think I am special in some ways because I can always make anyone laugh or have their heart fill with joy all over again.

If I could change anything about myself I would change that a girl I like a lot who has another boyfriend would like me more. I have set some goals for myself like trying to be as good a friend as I can to everybody, especially the girl I like, even though that is challenging sometimes.

When I was younger, if I could have, I would have changed the universe and re-arranged the planet's order, because I wanted to get a better look at Pluto, since no one had ever seen Pluto…but I couldn't do that. Now my dream for our planet and our world is that there would be peace, there is nothing more important than that.

I think the greatest day of my life was when I met my good friend at my school. The worse day of my life was the day she started dating another guy in my class, and it took me a whole year, maybe longer, but now I am o.k. with it because I recognize you can't stop true love.

One thing I know I have learned is that when some people look at people they might not always see that a person is really sweet or how beautiful they are because I see people from the inside out and some people only see others from the outside.

Once I gave a friend a ring and if I could change anything now it would be that I wouldn't have given her the ring because she never even wore jewelry and it hurt my heart that she gave it back to me.

A very sad thing that happened to me was when Natalie left. Natalie was my really good friend since first grade and we really liked each other and I really miss her. Sometimes I don't like to talk about the fact that we are divorced and I take growth hormone. I don't like to talk about those things because they make me feel sad.

Mom, you have influenced me a lot because you have taught me to always keep my chin up and maybe there will be a brighter future. You also taught me that although I like some girls they might not like me the same way, and that doesn't mean that they didn't want to be with me, or that I am weird. I would want the world to know that I am a really sweet person and not to judge me from the outside, but to judge me from the inside.

I am happiest when my friends appreciate me. I am happiest when I am at school with my friends or just hanging out with them. I am saddest when someone pushes me away. It makes me feel unwanted.

If I could meet anyone it would be Jackie Robinson because he was such an inspiration to baseball and he dealt with so much criticism and he was even pushed away by his own team mates but he was a great guy and he overcame his anger and he went on to become an amazing baseball hero.

If these were my last words, I would say, "Never give up, even when girls don't like you."

Cinnamon Snails

½ cup butter, softened
¾ cup packed brown sugar
1 teaspoon ground cinnamon
¼ teaspoon baking powder
1 egg
1 teaspoon vanilla extract

2 cups all purpose flour
1 tablespoon white sugar
½ teaspoon cinnamon
1 lightly beaten egg white
chocolate chips

Preheat oven to 375.

Beat butter for 30 seconds.

Add brown sugar, cinnamon, and baking powder; beat till combined.

Beat in egg and vanilla; add flour.

On a floured surface, shape each portion of dough into a 12-inch log.

Cut each log into 24 half-inch pieces. Roll each piece into a 6-inch rope.

Coil the ropes into a snail shape.

Place them 2 inches apart on a slightly greased cookie sheet.

Brush with egg white.

In a small bowl, stir sugar and cinnamon; sprinkle over the snails.

Use chocolate chips for the eyes.

Bake 8 minutes.

Remember even if they all don't look perfect,
they will all taste really good.

A NOTE ABOUT THE AUTHOR

Robyn Stecher is currently executive vice president at Don Buchwald and Associates, Inc., a bi-coastal talent agency.

In the early 1980s, Robyn convinced a former TV producer and longtime talent agent, that without her he'd be lost—and she became his assistant. This launched her twenty-two-year career in the entertainment industry and eventual nineteen-year association with her current firm, DBA. Her clients include many well-known actors and voice-over performers, as well as other television and film celebrities.

In 1991, soon after her son Daniel was born, Robyn was told he would be challenged with lifelong neurological impairment. Determined that neither of them were going to suffer or live damaged lives, she embraced her son's differences and capabilities. Today, Daniel is a thriving high school student. Once unintelligible, Daniel has overcome his severe speech impairment and has held student council positions. He barely handwrites, but he has mastered the computer and writes screenplays, has sung in chorus, won awards for his journalism, and was the recipient of the nationally recognized "Triple C Award" in 2006 for outstanding commitment, spirit, and involvement at The Lowell Middle School in Queens, New York. Daniel possesses encyclopedic knowledge of baseball and he dreams of working for a team one day. He also loves to bake.

Robyn's charitable contributions include her work on behalf of The Dream Foundation, based in California. She was selected as one of the 2003 Woman of The Year honorees for the foundation for her longtime commitment to making the dreams of terminally ill adults come true. Robyn began her work for The Dream Foundation in 1995 after her sister's life was lost to terminal cancer. She worked for nine years in service to the foundation's wish-granting efforts and its advisory board. Today, The Dream Foundation is the largest national wish-granting organization for terminally ill adults in the country and grants approximately one thousand dreams a year.

Robyn was instrumental in creating fund-raising initiatives for her son's special education school, The Lowell School in New York, and has served for six years as benefit co-chair and capital campaign committee member. In addition to her charitable activities, her varied interests have included years of writing, cooking, dancing, and a love of red wines. She also was once a world-class scuba diver.

A member of the New York Friar's Club since 2007, she resides on the Upper East Side of Manhattan with her son; her partner in love and life, Jim Weiss; and their dog, Gracie.

Robyn's greatest fulfillment comes from inspiring others to manifest the joy of embracing the unexpected and creating possibility. She is devoted to the quest of exploring potential and creating meaningful, empowered experiences in everyday life.

There's Something About Daniel is her first book.

LaVergne, TN USA
26 May 2010
184067LV00003B/201/P